C000062967

Snowdonia Walks with Children

Nick Lambert

SIGMA
Leisure

Published by Sigma Leisure – an imprint of
Sigma Press, 1 South Oak Lane, Wilmslow, Cheshire SK9 6AR, England.

British Library Cataloguing in Publication Data
A CIP record for this book is available from the British Library.

ISBN: 1-85058-614-4

Typesetting and Design by: Sigma Press, Wilmslow, Cheshire.

Printed by: MFP Design & Print

Cover photograph: the ferry from Fairbourne to Barmouth *(Graham Beech)*

Maps and photographs: Nick Lambert

Location map: Morag Perrott

Disclaimer: the information in this book is given in good faith and is believed to be correct at the time of publication. No responsibility is accepted by either the author or publisher for errors or omissions, or for any loss or injury howsoever caused. Only you can judge your own fitness, competence and experience.

Croeso (Welcome)

Most of my childhood holidays were spent in Wales, and perhaps it's there that I picked up my enthusiasm for walking. Although Snowdonia is known mainly for its spectacular mountain scenery, there are many areas in the impressive valleys that are ideal for families; either completely flat, or with only short climbs.

These walks have been chosen and written with children in mind, and cover the whole of Snowdonia, taking in a wide variety of the scenery available within the National Park. Some routes feature well-known beauty spots, others explore quieter, lesser-frequented areas, where it is possible to get away from it all and enjoy the peace of the countryside.

Most of the walks have "Escape Routes" so each family can tailor the walk to suit their time and energy. Ideal for those with very young, less enthusiastic children. Parking, toilets and suitable cafés and pubs along the route are listed, as are baby-changing facilities when available.

Each route is accompanied by a sketch map, photographs and details of other places to visit in the area.

Enjoy your walks!

Nick Lambert

	Rail	Bus	Cafe	Pubs	Flat	Features
Bala						
Lake Railway	–	✓	✓	✓	–	Lakeside railway, boat hire.
Lovers Walk	–	✓	✓	✓	–	Plenty of wildlife
Beddgelert:						
Gelert's Grave	–	✓	✓	✓	✓	The "grave" itself
Aberglaslyn	–	✓	–	–	–	Exciting walk through railway tunnel; not for the faint hearted
Beddgelert Forest	–	✓	✓	✓	–	Mountain views
Sygun	–	✓	✓	✓	–	Copper mine open to public
Betws-y-Coed:						
Riverside Walk	✓	✓	✓	✓	✓	Railway Museum
Miners Bridge	✓	✓	✓	✓	✓	Old miners' bridge over the river gorge
Llyn Elsi	✓	✓	✓	✓	–	Mountain views
Conwy:						
Quayside	✓	✓	✓	✓	–	Boat trips, seaside shops
Above Conwy	✓	✓	✓	–	–	Castle views
Dyfi Valley:						
Aberdyfi	✓	✓	✓	✓	–	Nice seaside town, boat trips etc
Pennal	–	✓	–	✓	–	Wild and windy riverside walk
Harlech:						
Harlech town	✓	✓	✓	✓	–	Castle, playground, beaches
Llandanwg	✓	✓	✓	–	–	Slate cavern open to public
River Artro	✓	✓	✓	✓	–	Gardens open to public, nearby Maes Artro Village and Shell Island
Llanberis:						
Dolbadarn	–	✓	✓	✓	–	Castle, 2 small railways, boats, waterfalls, museums, country park
Llyn Padarn	–	✓	✓	✓	–	Country park amenities, boats, steam train, nature centre
Mawddach Estuary:						
Barmouth	✓	✓	✓	✓	–	Beach and views
Barmouth/ Fairbourne	✓	✓	✓	✓	✓	Steam trains, optional boat ride, toll footbridge, crossing estuary, beach
Morfa Mawddach	✓	–	–	–	✓	Old railway path
Penmaenpool	–	✓	–	✓	–	Old railway path

Contents

Before you Begin . . .

Walks around Bala

Walks around Beddgelert

Walks around Betws-y-Coed

Walks around Conwy

Walks around The Dyfi Estuary

Walks around Harlech to Llanbedr

Walks around Llanberis

Walks around the Mawddach Estuary

50 Questions & Answers for Boring Journeys

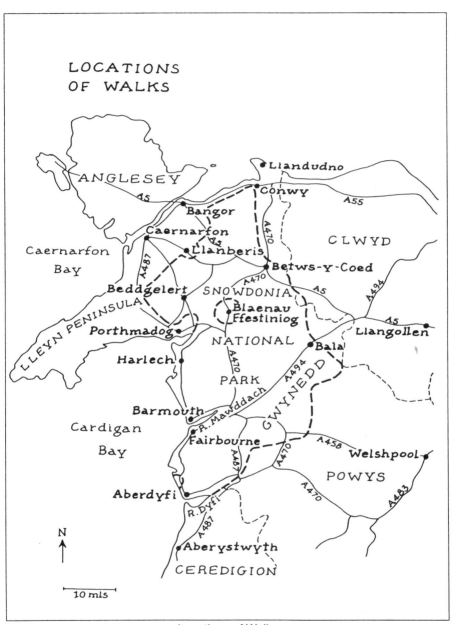

Locations of Walks

Before you Begin . . .

This book is intended to be read by both parents and children. The following conventions have been used to make the book easy to use:

1. Directions are numbered and can be seen at a glance.

☺ Information with the smiley face in the margin is for the children, to be read aloud, or for them to read themselves.

Questions (and **answers**) are in the same type style, but are preceded by "Q" and "A". These can be used by parents as quizzes along the way — it would have been too awkward to have placed the answers at the back of the book, involving much flicking between different parts of the book.

In between the instructions there is text that looks like this, which is used for all sorts of information, from background material to escape routes – generally, the sort of thing you can skate over if you are in a rush to complete the main walk.

Checklists appear at the end of each walk, for the child to tick off things as they see them. If you do not want to write in the book, copy out the checklist on a piece of paper, and give one to each child, so they can compete to see who spots the most.

Sketch Maps

The maps are intended only as a rough guide to the route and are not drawn to scale. Unless otherwise stated, north is upwards. Only buildings important to the route are shown. Numbers refer to the directions given in the text. On the maps, this is how the various features are denoted:

Roads	=	a continuous line
Footpaths	=	a dotted line
Trackways/forest roads/drive-ways	=	a line of dashes
Parking	=	P
Pubs	=	PH

1

The Country Code (and some other common-sense advice)

- ➲ Don't drop litter. If there is no bin, take it home with you.
- ➲ The countryside should be a place of peace and tranquillity. Do not ruin it for other people by shouting and screaming.
- ➲ Close all gates after you, otherwise you might cause flocks of sheep to stray onto the road and get run over.
- ➲ Keep dogs on leads when there are farm animals around, and keep them under close control at all times.
- ➲ Do not try to get too near to wild animals, as many of them will be frightened and may *bite*!
- ➲ If stroking farm animals such as horses, keep fingers *well away* from their mouths, or you may lose them.
- ➲ Always stick to the public footpaths/bridleways, and do not stray onto private land.
- ➲ Some farms use electric fences to separate fields. These are usually a single wire held up by occasional plastic supports. The charge is only low, and won't kill you. Even so, it's not a good idea to grab hold of them, as a shock can be alarming.
- ➲ Do not cross railway lines, except at authorised crossing places.
- ➲ Always walk on the right hand side of a lane or road, so that you are walking *towards* the traffic, so that you can see any approaching vehicle. Keep well into the side of the road and keep in single file. Restrain small children as traffic approaches.
- ➲ Do not pick wild flowers. Leave them for others to enjoy.
- ➲ Never eat wild berries. They may look colourful and tasty, like sweets, but many are deadly poisonous. The same goes for mushrooms and toadstools. No matter how nice and colourful they look, don't touch them.
- ➲ Never fool around near water. Do not paddle in a stream or pond unless an adult says it is safe to do so.
- ➲ Respect the countryside, and enjoy your walk!
- ➲ Please read the passages from this book while you are standing still, not walking, or it might be the last walk you go on.

A Note About Public Rights of Way

In many areas there are a lot of problems with farmers and landowners illegally blocking public footpaths. In Snowdonia, being a National Park, there are very few such problems. In fact, the only place

I had any trouble was the Dyfi Valley, where many of the footpaths have disappeared completely and where (according to a local man I met) the landowners have been blocking paths for twenty years. As a result, many of the walks I had planned in the area had to be scrapped, which is a great shame, because it is a beautiful valley.

Public Footpaths are in most cases ancient rights of way, and not even the landowner has the right to prevent their use. If you encounter hazards or blocked paths on your walk, then the Ramblers' Association would like to hear from you, but first, always double check the correct route of the right of way on an up-to-date Ordnance Survey map. You can contact the RA at: The Ramblers' Association, 1/5 Wandsworth Road, London   SW8 2XX

Public Transport

All Rail Enquiries: 0345 484950

Buses: Different bus companies operate the various services. Gwynedd County Council produce a handy booklet with details, maps, times and phone numbers, and this is available from Tourist Information Centres.

Tourist Information Centres

Use TICs to book accommodation or find out what's going on in the area. Many have interesting exhibits and displays. All are closed during the winter unless otherwise stated.

Aberdyfi (for the Dyfi valley): The Wharf Gardens. 01654 767321

Bala: Penllyn, Pensarn Road. 01678 521021

Barmouth (for the Mawddach Estuary): The Old Library. 01341 280787

Beddgelert: There is a small NT shop/information room. For further info see Betws-y-Coed TIC below.

Betws-y-Coed (open all year): The Stables. 01690 710426

Conwy (open all year): Castle Visitor Centre at the castle entrance. 01492 592248

Harlech: High Street. 01766 780658

Llanberis: High Street. 01286 870765

Glossary

Most signposts are in Welsh and English and most Welsh people speak English as well, but here is a handful of Welsh words which crop up frequently in place names, and a few other handy everyday words you might come across:

aber	river mouth
afon	river
araf	slow
bach	little
bedd	grave
betws	church
brenin	king
bryn	hill
capel	chapel
castell	castle
coed	woods
croeso	welcome
cwm	valley
dim parcio	no parking
llan	place or church
maes	field
nant	brook
newydd	new
parc	park
pentre	village
plas	hall
pont	bridge
porth	port/harbour
traeth	shore/beach
ynys	island

Walks around Bala

Bala is set amongst the gentle hills of eastern Snowdonia, on the A494. It is a solid and practical Welsh market town with plenty of cafés, pubs and restaurants in the town centre, and a couple of good eat-in chippies. There are plenty of amenities for the tourist, including a good information centre, near the lakeside car park, and a leisure centre with a swimming pool. Boats are available for hire on the lake, and of great interest to the visitor is the Bala Lake Railway, which runs along one side of the lake.

Bala: the lake

Bala: Bala Lake and Railway

A moderate walk, one way only, with the chance to return via one of the steam trains on the Bala Lake Railway. (Check train times before setting off. Leaflets are available from the TIC close to the start of the route.) There are good views of the lake and a more rugged and open side to the area can be explored.

Starting Point: Lake car park, just south of Bala town centre, off the A494. (SH921355). Well-signed. Alternatively, start from Llangower station, off the B4403 on the south side of the lake, where there is a car park, toilets and picnic site. Catch the train to Bala station and begin the return walk from Direction 6.

By Bus: Buses to Bala town centre from Barmouth (rail connection), Dolgellau and Wrexham.

Car Parking: At both Starting Points.

Distance: Entire route from Bala: 5½ miles.

Terrain: Half the walk is uphill, though none of the climbs are too strenuous. May be boggy after heavy rain.

Maps: OS Landranger 125, OS Outdoor Leisure 18 or 23.

Public Toilets: At Lake car park (Starting Point), and Llangower car park (finish).

Refreshments: Café at Lake car park, café at Leisure Centre passed en route. Nothing after that. (At the Lakeside car park there are toilets, and a small café with outdoor seating available and boats for hire.)

---

1.   **At the back of the car park there is a raised footpath. Steps lead up to it next to the toilet block. Bear right, so the lake is on your right. (Alternatively, just follow the rough trackway along the shoreline, but when it becomes impassable, join the footpath via any of the steps or the ramp.)**

☺   This is Bala Lake, which in Welsh is known as "Llyn Tegid". ("Llyn" means lake.) The lake is nearly four miles long, and from here there are good views across the water. For even better views look out for the "telescope" which you should soon pass.

The building on the left of the footpath houses the TIC, so check train times now if you haven't already. After the TIC is a leisure centre, open daily, where there is a swimming pool and café.

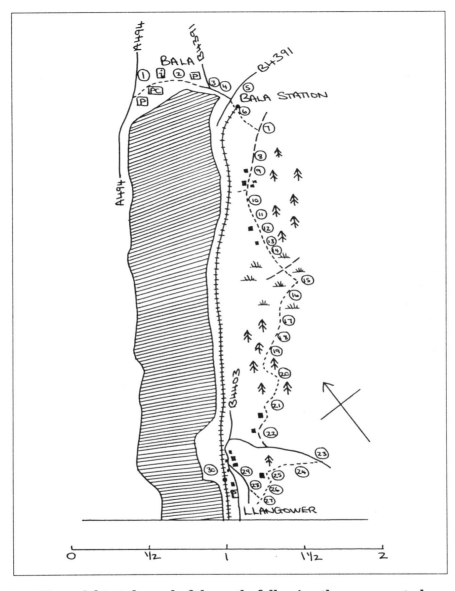

2. **Keep right at the end of the path, following the pavement along the lakeshore.**

☺ To the right there are reeds and bushes growing close to the water's edge. These make a good place for birds to hide and nest.

3.   Keep right and cross the bridge over the river.

Q: Look at the road sign as you cross the bridge. Which direction is Llangower, right or left?

A: Right. That's where this walk finishes and you can catch the train back again.

4.   Keep right and cross the old stone bridge.

☺ This bridge is very old and no longer has traffic going over it, only walkers. If you look over the wall there is (usually) no water underneath it now. It has two arches.

5.   Carefully cross the road and go through the kissing gate opposite, signed as a footpath and for the Bala Lake Railway. Follow the path up to the station.

☺ This is Bala Station, which is the start of the Bala Lake Railway. The line was once used to carry slate from quarries in North Wales. Today it is used for pleasure, and small steam trains carry tourists along the side of the lake.

The line was reopened by local businessmen and steam enthusiasts. It originally ran from Ruabon to Morfa Mawddach, near Fairbourne. The latter stretch of the line is now a footpath, see the Morfa Mawddach walk.

The lake from Llangower Station

☺ If you look under the bridge you will see old signs advertising dog biscuits and Fry's chocolate, very different from today's adverts.

6. **Cross over the footbridge and go through the gate on the other side. Bear diagonally right across the field, leading slightly uphill. Cross the stile towards the top right hand corner of the field. Keep right along the edge of the field.**

☺ To the right you should have views of the lake. To the left, through the trees, you might be ale to see a campsite, where there might be tents and caravans. See how many tents you can count.

7. **Climb the stile at the end of the field and bear right along the trackway. Avoid the footpath into the woods.**

☺ There are nettles and other wild plants growing on both sides of the path now, and uphill on the left are the tall trees of a forest. Look out for fir cones on the ground. You may also see squirrels or wild rabbits running for cover.

8. **The track passes behind farm buildings. Go through the gate barring the track and continue ahead.**

☺ Look out for the prickly gorse bushes along the track now, which have yellow flowers in the summer. The thorns are very sharp, so take care as you pass them.

9. **The track passes behind a hotel. Where it splits bear right, signed with a yellow arrow, leading slightly downhill. The path splits again around an island of trees, then rejoins. About 15 yards after the path has rejoined look out for a signed footpath leading off to the left, which might be partially hidden in undergrowth. Follow the clear path through the trees and bushes, which keeps fairly level. Do not bear off uphill to the left. The path drops back down to the golf course. Keep ahead along the edge of the green.**

10. **Towards the end of the green look out for the stile in the fence. Cross over and continue straight ahead.**

Q: Look out for goats in the fields on the right now. Do you know the names for a male and a female goat?

A: The females are called "nanny goats." The males are called "billy goats".

11. **Keep ahead along this path, with a fence on your right. Don't go**

through any gateways to the right, and don't be drawn uphill into the woods, where there is a stile and sign.

☺ There are nettles in places along the path now, which, as I'm sure you'll know, can sting you. Also there are more of those thorny bushes with the yellow flowers. Can you remember what they are called?

12. **When you reach the fenced woodland ahead, with a stream running through it, bear right and follow the fence downhill. At the bottom bear left, crossing the stream, after which the path starts to lead uphill again. Keep with the fence on the right now, leading away from the stream.**

13. **Cross over the stile and bear left, uphill. The path winds between bracken and boulders, but make sure you keep the fence in sight on your left. As you get higher the path becomes more clearly defined.**

☺ The walk now crosses wild, open moorland, where it can be quite windy. There are few trees now, and little else grows except grass.

Q: There will probably be many sheep grazing on the grass. Do you know the names for a male and female sheep?

A: A male is called a "ram" and a female is called a "ewe".

14. **You should come across a narrow stream on your left, which you want to follow all the way up to the trackway. At the trackway bear right. Go through the metal gate on the left and follow the stony trackway leading uphill, with a fence on your right.**

☺ You are quite high up now and there are good views over the lake to the town of Bala, where the walk started. Amongst the chimneys and rooftops see if you can spot a church spire.

15. **At the ladder stile climb over and follow the clear pathway downhill through the bracken.**

☺ Take care not to slip as you are going downhill. You should be able to see the lake in the distance, which you are heading towards. Can you see any boats on the water? Also see if you can see a campsite close to the lake shore.

16. **Keep to the main path leading downhill. Cross the small stream and continue ahead, still towards the lake.**

17. **Go through the gateway barring the track and continue ahead, signed for the lake.**

☺ These trees are mainly oaks, from which acorns come. In the autumn you will probably see hundreds of acorns on the ground. They are the seeds of the oak, and if they fall in soil can grow into a new tree.

18. **When you come to the stile climb over. You now need to cross the stream and climb the ladder stile opposite. (There are a set of rough steps leading down to the stream, but it might be safer to go downstream a few yards and make your own way across.)**

☺ Animals you might see on your walk include: a cow, a sheep, a goat, a horse, a duck, a swan, a goose, a squirrel, a rabbit and many different types of insects from bees to beetles, not forgetting butterflies and spiders.

19. **After the ladder stile continue ahead across the field, with your back to the stream. In the middle of the field bear left and follow the grassy trackway uphill. (If you have reached a further stream before bearing left uphill, you've gone too far.) At the top of the field is a crumbling drystone wall. Go around or over this and bear right with the fence on your left. Continue ahead, following the fence. The path becomes a very clear trackway, at which point someone has thoughtfully put an arrow, now you no longer need one.**

20. **Follow the trackway downhill through the woods.**

(Keep an eye on young children, as the woods drop down on the right.)

☺ You should be able to see the lake occasionally between the trees. Do you notice how it is getting nearer all the time?

21. **Go through the metal gate barring the track and continue ahead. Keep right, heading towards the buildings. Go through the gateway and down the trackway towards the farm, but bear off to the left, passing behind the buildings. Keep up on the left passing the rural farmhouse, complete with satellite dish. When you come to the farm driveway bear left. Beware of any vehicles now.**

Q: There are fields to the right, which usually have sheep in them. What is a young sheep called?

A: A lamb.

22. At the lane bear left.

Escape route: For emergencies only, as the road at the bottom is narrow and winding. Bear right along this lane, and left at the bottom. Take care crossing the bridge. The station and car park are on the right after the church.

☺ Down on your right there is a stream, which carries water down from the hills to the lake. In turn the water from the lake flows along a river to join the sea near Barmouth. All rivers eventually lead to the sea. Perhaps you have a river near where you live. Do you know where it joins the sea?

23. After a third of a mile you should come to a gravel trackway leading off to the right. About 35 yards after this is a footbridge. Cross over and bear right and return to the trackway. Begin to follow the trackway as it leads uphill, but on the hairpin bend keep ahead along the grassy pathway leading above the stream.

24. Keep straight ahead and climb the series of ladder stiles. The path is very easy to follow at this point.

☺ Look at the ground for footprints in the mud, if there is any. You will probably see bootprints left by other walkers, but there may also be prints left by animals such as sheep, cows or dogs, or even tiny prints left by birds.

25. Bear left, signed with a yellow arrow, before the farm buildings. The path leads uphill over a rough grassy area. Keep to the middle of this field. There are occasional arrows to show the way, leading to a ladder stile at the top under a tree.

26. Continue straight ahead after the stile, following the remains of a row of trees which once divided the fields.

☺ You should have a good view of the lake on your right. It isn't much further now, honestly!

27. At the end of the field, if you've kept with the tree stumps, a clear pathway will lead you down to a plank bridge over a stream. Climb the ladder stile on the other side and follow the clear path uphill. At the top bear right, through the gateway, and follow the stream downhill.

☺ Like I said, it isn't much further now, and you might be pleased to hear that it's downhill all the way from now on.

28. Climb the stile next to the gate at the bottom. Bear right along the quiet lane.

Q: There are hedges along the sides of the lane, which will have many wild plants and flowers growing in them. Can you think of a prickly animal which is well known for living in hedges?

A: A hedgehog

☺   At the bottom of this lane there is a little church, with a small graveyard. There is a bell in the tower on the roof of the church. On a Sunday, the bell is rung to tell the villagers that a service is about to start.

29. Bear left along the lane at the bottom, taking great care. Go through the car park on the right.

(At the entrance to the car park there is a toilet block. There are picnic tables scattered around and access to the shore of the lake.)

30. At the back of the car park there is a gate which leads to Llangower station. Take care crossing the tracks to the platform.

Bala Lake & Railway Checklist

☐ A SEAGULL

☐ A BOAT WITH A SAIL

☐ A DOG

☐ A STONE BRIDGE

☐ A TENT

☐ A TRAIN

☐ A SHEEP

☐ A TREE WITH RED BERRIES

☐ A COW

☐ A WHITE STONE COTTAGE

☐ A GOAT

☐ A RAILWAY SIGNAL

Bala: "The Lovers' Walk"

An Easy to Moderate walk. A couple of minutes' walk and the bustle of Bala town centre is left behind. This is a really pleasant and attractive short route.

Starting Point: The Green car park, (SH929361). Well-signed from the main road. Signed for parking and Bala Lake Railway

By Bus: Buses to Bala town centre from Barmouth, Dolgellau and Wrexham.

Car Parking: At the Starting Point, and various other well-signed places.

Distance: 3 miles.

Terrain: Footpaths and quiet lanes, no serious uphill stretches.

Maps: OS Landranger 125, OS Outdoor Leisure 18 or 23.

Public Toilets: Town centre

Refreshments: Town centre.

---

1.   **From the car park bear right along the road towards the main street, then right again, passing the Fire Station on the right and cross over the bridge. (Bear left instead of right for the town centre, shops, cafés etc)**

Q: Look out for the triangular sign close to the bridge with a horse and rider on it. What do you think this means?

A: Triangular road signs tend to be warnings. This one is warning motorists that there might be horses being ridden along this road, so they should take care.

2.   **After the bridge, carefully cross the road, bearing right along the pavement, passing the castellated entrance to a stately home. Cross over the narrow lane and continue ahead along the footpath, running parallel with the road.**

Q: Look out for the big road sign. How many miles is it to Llangollen?

A: 21.

3.   **Beneath the large oak tree take the footpath off to the left, climbing the stile over the fence and keep to the left of the field. Keep straight ahead and avoid any gates leading off.**

☺ There might be sheep in these fields. See if you can spot any tufts of their wool on the ground. Most sheep are white, but you can sometimes see black or brown ones.

"Castellated gateway" just outside the town of Bala

4. **Climb the stile at the end of the field and continue straight ahead, starting to lead uphill for a short way. At the top of the field head for the gate. Next to it is another stile. Cross over and bear right, with the fence on your right.**

Escape route: To cut a corner off the route continue straight ahead after the stile until you join the lane. Here bear left and continue from Direction 7.)

☺ This is called the "Lovers' Walk". Notice there are trees planted in rows and there are good views to both sides. The trees are mainly oaks, which have "acorns" in the autumn. An acorn is the seed of the oak, and if planted will grow into a young tree.

5. **The path starts to lead downhill. Go through the gate and bear left along the quiet lane. As always, be aware of any approaching vehicles. (Try not to notice the sub-station on the left.) Continue ahead.**

Q: There are hedgerows on both sides of the lane, made up of many different types of plant, including brambles, foxgloves, ivy, nettles, grasses and ferns. One of these plants has a purple bell-shaped flower in spring and summer. Do you know which one?

A: Foxgloves. They are also poisonous, so don't touch them.

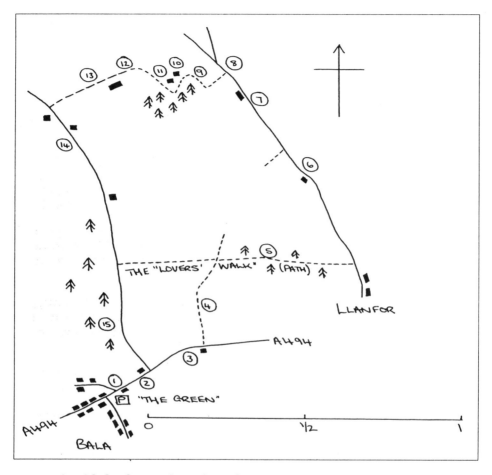

6.   **Avoid the footpath to the left.**

7.   **Continue ahead along the lane, passing the stone houses on the left.**

Q: Very soon the lane ahead splits in two. The turning to the right has a "T" sign next to it. What do you think this means?

A: The road is a dead end; it doesn't lead anywhere.

8.   **Before the lane splits bear left through the metal gateway, currently unsigned. Continue straight ahead, leading slightly down-**

hill, towards the lone oak tree. After this bear right, with a hedgerow and wall on your immediate left.

☺ There are good views ahead, and look out for glimpses of the lake in the distance.

9. This is where it gets complicated. Keeping left, a path leads alongside the hedge, down a dip and between some stone gate-posts to a stream. Cross the stream via the stone slab bridge towards the ruins of some old cottages.

☺ These buildings are in ruins. The roofs have fallen in and some of the walls are falling down. Ruins like these can be very dangerous, so you should never play in them, no matter how interesting they might look.

10. After the bridge bear left, passing the nearest building on your right, continuing under the branches of the trees until you come to the fenced woodland. Bear right and follow the fence to the small stile.

11. Cross over the stile, cross over the ditch and bear left initially, alongside the woodland, but start to veer to the right, towards a gate in the fence ahead. Go through the gate and continue straight ahead.

☺ The roofs of farm buildings should come into view ahead, and again you might be able to see the lake occasionally, between the buildings.

12. Go through the gateway underneath the sycamore tree and continue straight ahead, avoiding gateways to either side.

Q: There are often cows in these fields. Do you know what cows eat?
A: That's an easy one. It's all around you: grass.

13. Go through the long wooden gate at the end and bear right along the farm driveway. Bear left along the lane.

☺ Pass the brick cottages on your right, which have many tall chimney pots and wild roses climbing up the walls. Soon you should pass more buildings on your left, with a huge gateway in the middle which looks as though it might lead into a castle. This is a stable block, where horses live. On the roof above the gate there is a "weathervane" which shows which way the wind is blowing. The weathervane has a horse on it.

14. Follow the lane all the way back to the main road.

☺ You might be pleased to hear that it is flat or downhill all the way back now. There are good views to the left over the fields and woodlands you have walked through.

In the woods on the right there are usually many wild birds. Even if you can't see any you might be able to hear them singing in the treetops.

15. **Bear right along the pavement of the main road, crossing the bridge again and returning to the car park and Starting Point.**

Bala: "The Lovers' Walk" Checklist

☐ A CHURCH SPIRE

☐ A CHURCH TOWER

☐ A SHEEP

☐ A HORSE

☐ A COW

☐ A DOG

☐ A TRACTOR

☐ A PINK FLOWER

☐ A STONE BRIDGE

☐ A BLACK BIRD

Walks around Beddgelert

Beddgelert is set in the middle of north Snowdonia, in the shadow of Snowdon itself, seven miles north of Porthmadog. It is an attractive stone village at the confluence of two rivers, the Colwyn and the Glaslyn, surrounded by dramatic mountain scenery. Popular with tourists, but thankfully not spoilt by them. Famous for the legend of Gelert, the faithful hound of the medieval prince, Llewelyn the Great. The dog's supposed grave is situated close to the river, to which visitors flock like pilgrims to a refectory. (See "Gelert's Grave walk".)

There are plans to reinstate the Welsh Highland Railway which once ran through the village, in which case it will be accessible by rail from Caernarfon and will link with the Ffestiniog Railway at Porthmadog, but these plans have been met locally by opposition.

Beddgelert: the village

Apart from walking, you can don a helmet and explore the old Sygun Copper Mine. (See Sygun walk for more details.) There are several craft shops and galleries around the village and no shortage of restaurants, cafés and pubs. Plenty of hotels and a couple of campsites.

Beddgelert: Gelert's grave

Beddgelert: Gelert's Grave

This easy, short walk is very popular, as tourists flock to see the grave of Prince Llewelyn's hound, Gelert. A very easy route with no climbing whatsoever, attractive scenery and a legend thrown in for good measure. What more could you ask for?

Starting Point: The car park, Beddgelert. (SH588481) off the A498, well signed.

By Bus: Services from Porthmadog and Carnaerfon.

Car Parking: Starting Point, village car park.

Distance: 1 mile.

Terrain: Easy. Completely flat, no climbs whatsoever. Riverside footpaths.

Maps: OS Landranger 115, OS Outdoor Leisure 17

Public Toilets: Beddgelert village, well signed.

Refreshments: Various places in the village

Pushchairs: The first part of the walk along the river is ideal. The return journey is a bit bumpy, but easily passable, though there are a few kissing gates to contend with.

---

1. From the car park, bear left onto the main village street and follow it into the village. Where the road bears left and crosses the bridge over the river, keep straight ahead along a smaller road, signed for "Gelert's Grave", with the river on your left and various craft shops on the right.

Q: Look out for a plaque on the right with daffodils on it. In which year did this village win the "Wales in Bloom" competition?

A: 1993.

The toilets are at the end of this road on the right.

Q: Look for the Keep Wales Tidy Competition plaque, which the village won in 1991. What kind of creature does it have on it?

A: A red dragon.

2. Directly after the toilet block take the gate on the right before the metal bridge and follow the riverside path.

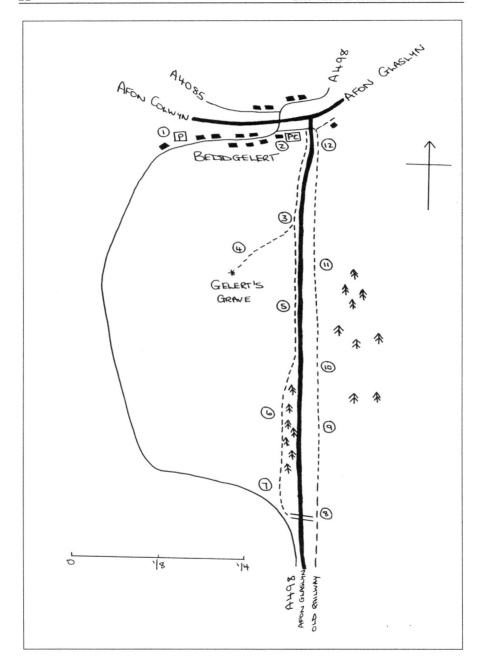

☺ This is the River Glaslyn, or "afon" Glaslyn in Welsh, which is wide and shallow at this point. It joins the sea near the town of Porthmadog.

There might be sheep in this field. Can you see any black ones?

3. **After a short way, bear right, signed again for "Gelert's Grave" and follow the path to the grave.**

☺ Once upon a time, a very long time ago, Llywelyn, the Prince of North Wales had his palace in this area. One day he returned home, and Gelert, his faithful dog, ran to meet him, but Gelert was covered in fresh blood. In horror, the Prince ran to the cot where his baby son should have been lying, but the cot was empty and there was blood on the blankets. Thinking the worst, Llywelyn took his sword and plunged it into Gelert's heart, killing him. The Prince stared at the body of poor Gelert, and then heard a cry from another room, where he found his baby son alive, and there on the floor was the body of a wolf. Gelert had saved the Prince's son from the wolf, and his only reward was to be killed by his master. Llewelyn was overcome with sadness, and it is said that he never smiled again. The village is named after Gelert. In Welsh, Beddgelert means "Gelert's Grave" and this is supposed to be that grave.

But those in the know doubt that any of this is true and believe that the tale was concocted to bring tourists, such as us, flocking to the village. So far, it seems to have worked well.

4. **Return the same way to the main path and continue along the river.**

Escape route: *Bear left and return to the village the same way.*

☺ If you look to the right, you have a view towards Gelert's Grave in the middle of the field, surrounded by its fence and trees.

5. **Go through the gate and continue along the riverside path. Soon there is an area of fenced woodland on the left. Continue ahead.**

☺ This is a very popular place to walk. You will probably see people walking their dogs, people with rucksacks, people with walking sticks, and people with pushchairs with very young children in, who cannot walk yet.

6. **Go through a further gate, cross the small stream and continue ahead.**

☺ Ahead, up the bank is a road, you might be able to see cars passing. Can you see the bridge carrying the road? At one time a railway line passed under it, but it is no longer used and the tracks have been taken away and will have been melted down and made into new things.

7. Bear left and cross the bridge.

☺ This bridge once carried the West Highland Railway across the river. Today it is only used by people on foot. Originally, the railway ran right through the mountains from Caernarfon to Porthmadog. Perhaps you have visited these towns?

8. Bear left along the edge of the river.

Alternatively, for a longer walk bear right and follow the old railway line to Aberglaslyn where the river cuts through a deep wooded gorge. See also the Aberglaslyn route.

☺ There may be sheep again, so take care not to startle them. After a short way, the houses of the village should come into view across the river.

9. Keep close to the river at all times.

☺ There are many rocks and boulders lying around the path, which have fallen down from the hillside, probably hundreds of years ago. As you can see, the side of the hill is covered with loose rocks which are lying in heaps.

Q: The trees around the bottom of the hill are mainly oaks. What is the "fruit" of the oak tree?

A: The acorn.

10. Go through the gate and continue ahead, still along the river.

☺ There are prickly gorse bushes in places now, which have strong smell-ing flowers in the summer. They have very sharp thorns, so take care when passing them.

Perhaps you have heard of Rupert Bear? You may have done, because he was very popular at one time and famous for his yellow scarf and trousers. Alfred Bestall, who drew Rupert, lived nearby and used much of the countryside around you in his drawings.

11. Go through the kissing gate and continue ahead.

☺ Just after the gate on the right is a small area set aside as a wildlife meadow and picnic area, which has been planted with certain grasses, bushes and trees which will hopefully attract birds and butterflies. If it is summer, see if you can spot any butterflies hovering above the flowers.

12. Cross the footbridge and follow the road straight ahead into the village centre.

☺ In the village, look out for an inn sign showing a picture of the dog, Gelert, killing the wolf, and the Prince's son safely in his cradle. It should be on your left as you return to the car park.

Gelert's Grave Checklist

☐ THOMAS THE TANK ENGINE

☐ A WHITE CAR

☐ A BRIDGE OVER A RIVER

☐ A BRIDGE OVER A ROAD

☐ A SHEEP

☐ A GRAVESTONE

☐ A CHURCH BELL

☐ A PURPLE FLOWER (IN SUMMER)

☐ A YELLOW FLOWER (IN SUMMER)

☐ AN ACORN (IN WINTER)

☐ SOMEONE WALKING WITH A RUCKSACK

☐ SOMEONE WALKING WITH A DOG

Beddgelert: Beddgelert Forest

The whole route is quite long, but there are several Escape Routes, so it can be cut short at various points. Take sandwiches and drinks for a whole day out. Even in the winter there is plenty of colour and variety in the forest and several good viewpoints. There are numbered posts at every junction to help you find your way. Mountain bikes are available from deep within the forest, call 01766 890310.

Starting Point: The main car park, Beddgelert (SH588481). Well signed from the A498, close to the centre of the village.

By Bus: Services from Porthmadog and Caernarfon.

Car Parking: At Starting Point, village car park.

Distance: 6 miles.

Terrain: Moderate. Mainly gravelled forest trackways. Uphill stretches are fairly gradual.

Maps: OS Outdoor Leisure 17. OS Landranger 115.

Public Toilets: Beddgelert Village only.

Refreshments: Village only.

---

1. Head out of the car park, passing Thomas the Tank Engine and continuing to the main road. Bear right towards the hotel.

Q: Ahead of you is a large hotel named after an animal. What is it called?

A: The Royal Goat Hotel. Look out for the sculptures of goats on and around the building.

2. Bear right in front of the hotel, so you pass the side of it on your left. As the road bears left keep straight ahead along the stony trackway, leading behind the row of houses. Bear left, signed as a public footpath. The track curves around to the left, leading slightly uphill.

3. Continue straight ahead between the houses, cross over the road and continue along the path, which leads behind the garages, signed occasionally. Cross the bridge and go through the kissing gate. Bear right and follow the grassy track between stone walls.

☺ If you are tall enough to see over the stone wall on your right you should be able to see the rooftops of the village, and also the car park where you might have parked. Also look out for the school and football goal posts.

4. **Avoid gateways off to either side. Continue ahead. The path bears around, so there is a stream on your right. Follow the stony track leading slightly uphill to the ladder stile. Climb this, cross the bridge over the stream and bear left along the lane. (Beware of any farm traffic on the lane.)**

5. **Pass all the farm buildings and follow the trackway straight ahead into the trees, where there is a crossroads. (The left path leads only to the stream.) Bear right through the trees.**

☺ This path was once a railway line, which ran through the mountains between the Welsh towns of Caernarfon and Porthmadog. It was used to carry slate, which is a hard stone which is quarried in many places in Wales. Look around you, most of the grey stone you can see is slate. It can be used for many things, including making floor and roof tiles and building walls.

6. **Climb the ladder stile and continue along the old railway.**

☺ The railway has been closed for a very long time and during the Second World War the tracks were taken up so the metal could be melted down and re-used. There are plans to repair the railway and have passenger trains using it. This would be a nice way to travel through the mountains and would mean people wouldn't need to use their cars as much, but trains can be noisy and many footpaths, such as this one, might be lost. What do you think?

7. **Keep to the old railway trackbed, climb the ladder stile and cross the stream. This is now the start of Beddgelert Forest. Look out for the first of the numbered Posts, which is number 13. Continue straight ahead.**

☺ You should soon see a camp site on your left. See how many caravans you can count.

8. **Keep straight ahead at Post 12, passing the picnic site to the left of the path.**

9. **Continue straight ahead at the crossroads (Post 2) crossing the bridge. Follow the trackway, leading very slightly uphill. Keep**

left, avoiding the turning off to the right, and pass posts 3, 4, 5 and 6.

This river is the afon Mellionen. "afon" is Welsh for river. After heavy rain the river can be very full and fast flowing, bringing all the water down from the mountains. This river eventually joins the sea near Porthmadog.

Most of the trees in the forest are "conifers", which means they have their seeds in cones, so look for cones on the ground, which you can take home with you. Conifers have dark "needles" instead of flat leaves, and many of them are "evergreen", which means they don't lose their leaves in the autumn. If you are here in the autumn though, you will see that not all the conifers are evergreens. One type, the "larch", turns a yellow or pale brown colour.

Escape route: To cut the route shorter, bear right at Post 6 and follow the trackway uphill. At the junction (Post 7) bear left and continue from Direction 16.)

Q: Look out for Post 6

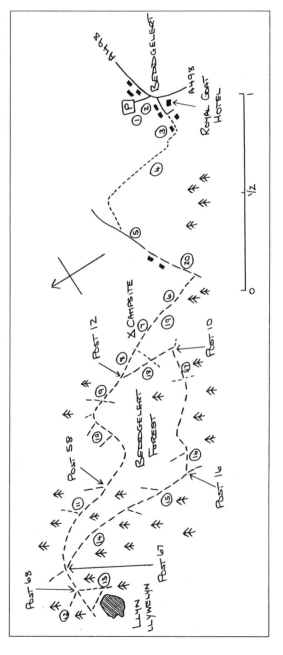

alongside the trackway. Soon after it there are small fields up on the left where there might be sheep or cows. The stone wall along the edge of the field is covered with ivy, brambles, mosses and ferns. Which of these plants has berries?

A: Brambles, which are also called blackberries.

10.   At the next junction (Post 82) continue ahead. After that bear left at Post 58. This path is narrower, leading uphill.

☺ At one time this whole area was a bare and rocky place, but it became a forest in 1926, when the first trees were planted. Forests are planted for their wood, and conifers are usually grown because they are fairly fast growing and can be planted quite close together. Where the trees are very close no light can reach the forest floor and it is quite dark, so nothing is able to grow, because all plants need sunlight to live.

11.   Pass Post 79 and continue ahead, avoiding the narrow path off to the right leading downhill. At the crossroads (Post 67) continue straight ahead.

Escape route: This will cut a corner off the route and save you a brief climb, but you'll miss the best part of the walk if you do, so be warned! Bear left at Post 67 and continue from Direction 14.

Q: Do you know what the tall, straight part of a tree is called?

A: The "bough" or "trunk".

12.   At the crossroads (Post 68) bear left crossing over the stream. At Post 73 bear right and follow the pathway along the lakeshore.

☺ This is Llyn Llywelyn. "Llyn" is Welsh for lake, and Llywelyn was a prince who lived in the area. There are good views across the lake and it is a nice place to stop for a while and have a rest. This is now the furthest part of the walk.

There are several picnic tables close to the lakeshore.

13.   At Post 69 bear right, leading downhill. This will return you to the crossroads (Post 68). Continue straight across. At Post 67 bear right.

☺ Along this path there are views over the treetops down into the valley below, and you can see the trees of the forest stretching away into the distance.

14. **Pass Posts 77 and 76. Pass Post 15 and continue ahead, avoiding the turning to the left.**

☺ There are different types of conifers growing in the forest, and they all have different types of cone, some small, some quite large. See how many different cones you can find on the ground.

Q: Occasionally you should get views straight ahead to the bare rocky mountain top of Moel Hebog, which means "Mountain of the Falcon". What is a "falcon"?

A: A type of bird.

15. **At Post 16 bear left, leading steadily downhill. At the T-junction (Post 7) bear right.**

☺ This is a working forest, which means that sometimes fully grown trees are cut down for their wood, and new trees are planted. The young trees are the same sort that you might have at Christmas. If it is a windy day listen as you are passing some tall, fully grown trees. The wind in the branches can sound like the rushing of a waterfall.

You should soon come to another field on your left, where again there might be sheep. There are views from here over the farmland to the lower parts of the forest.

16. **Keep to the main gravelled pathway. Where the path splits (Post 8), bear left along the lower trackway.**

☺ The path now starts to lead downhill. See if you can spot any cars driving along the main road in the valley. As you get lower down the rooftops and chimneys of the village should come into view in the distance.

17. **At Post 10 bear left, following the trackway past Post 11.**

Q: Look to the farmhouse up on the left. How many chimneys are there on the main roof?

A: Two.

18. **Continue to Post 12 on the outskirts of the campsite. Here bear right and return along the course of the old railway track, passing Post 13. Cross the stream, climb the ladder stile and continue along the trackbed.**

☺ You are now walking along the old railway line again. In a short way there are views to the right of a rocky hillside. After heavy rain there will be several gushing streams running down it.

19. Go through the gate/over the ladder stile and into the woods. Follow the path leading slightly downhill towards the stream. Bear left at the crossroads, following the trackway downhill towards the farm buildings.

Q: How many chimneys are there on the main roof of the first house?

A: ·Three.

Riverside pathway with part of the forest in the background

20. Follow the lane alongside the stream. Once past the last of the buildings cross the bridge over the stream and climb the ladder stile. Follow the rocky path to the left which runs with the stream for a way before bearing to the right to become the grassy trackway between stone walls. Go through the kissing gate at the end and follow the footpath down through the houses back to the village and starting point.

Beddgelert Forest Checklist

- ☐ A SQUIRREL
- ☐ A FALLEN TREE
- ☐ A FIRCONE
- ☐ A SHEEP
- ☐ A MOUNTAIN BIKE
- ☐ A BRIDGE
- ☐ A TENT
- ☐ A DOG
- ☐ A TRACTOR
- ☐ A YELLOW FLOWER

Beddgelert: Sygun Copper Mine

A walk of two distinct parts. The first half is flat, and apart from one ladder stile to negotiate it is acceptable for pushchairs, along a riverside path and a quiet lane. Those with pushchairs or a lack of energy return to the village the same way after Sygun Copper Mine, where refreshments are available, and there are trips down the mine. The second half of the walk involves some degree of effort, and stout shoes or boots are essential. Note that the paths are rocky and some scrambling is necessary in places, and some might consider this walk unsuitable for small children, so please use your discretion.

Starting point: The main car park, Beddgelert village, (SH588481), well signed off the A498

By Bus: From Porthmadog and Caernarfon. Both stop in the village centre.

Distance: 3 miles.

Terrain: As mentioned above, the first half of this walk is flat and very easy going, following footpaths and a quiet lane. The second half requires some degree of effort and follows a rocky path uphill, with some scrambling at the top, and a winding rocky descent back to the village. Care must be taken with younger children.

Maps: OS Landranger 115, OS Outdoor Leisure 17.

Public Toilets: In the village, close to the start of the route.

Refreshments: Various places in the village.

---

1. **From the car park follow the entrance driveway back to the main road and bear left, following the main street through the village. Where the road bears left and crosses the bridge over the river keep straight ahead along a smaller road, signed for Gelert's Grave. The river should be on your left.**

The public toilets are on the right at the end of this road.

Q: Look for a slate plaque with a red dragon on it. It tells you which year the village won the Keep Wales Tidy competition. Which year was it?

A: 1991.

2. **At the end of the road cross the bridge over the river.**

Q: This is Glaslyn Bridge, which crosses over the river or "afon" Glaslyn.

The river Colwyn joins it from the left. Which year was the bridge built?
Look for the plaque.

A: 1951

3.   **After the footbridge keep left, following the riverside path as it passes the row of cottages. Continue ahead, crossing over a driveway (but do not cross the bridge).**

Escape route: To return to the centre of the village cross the bridge and bear left.

4.   **Continue ahead through the gate and follow the riverside path.**

Q: Next to the gate is the sign for the "Snowdonia National Park" which this village is a part of. What flowers are shown on the plaque?

A: Daffodils, which are the emblem of Wales. The mountain in the background is, of course, Snowdon, which is the highest mountain in England and Wales. (Ben Nevis in Scotland is higher).

5.   **Follow the gravel path. The river should be over on your left.**

☺   The large bushes growing along the path are called "rhododendrons". They have large, dark green oval leaves and have lilac flowers in the summer. Lilac is a shade of purple. You will pass many rhododendrons on this walk.

6.   **Climb the ladder stile and bear right along the lane. This is a very quiet lane, but do be alert for any possible vehicles.**

Escape route: Bear left along the lane, crossing the bridge, then bear left again along the road back to be village.)

☺   This is a very pleasant country lane, with many wild plants growing at its sides, including bluebells in the spring and yellow poppies in the summer. Soon you should be able to see the river Glaslyn winding through the fields below, where there may be sheep and horses. Also there is a campsite. See how many tents you can count, and look out for the pond on the campsite where there are often ducks and geese.

Q: Look out for an old slate milepost on the left. How far is it to Beddgelert from here, and how far to Criccieth?

A: According to the milepost Beddgelert is half a mile away and Criccieth is 10½ miles. (Tremadog is 6 miles away and Capel Curig 12 miles.)

☺   Look out for an old stone house on the right with a weathervane on the top of the garage. A weathervane shows which way the wind is blowing. This weathervane has a cockerel on the top of it.

7.   Where the road ends go through the gate and continue ahead along the stony trackway between grass and bracken.

Q: On the left is the back of a white cottage. How many chimneys does it have?

A: Two.

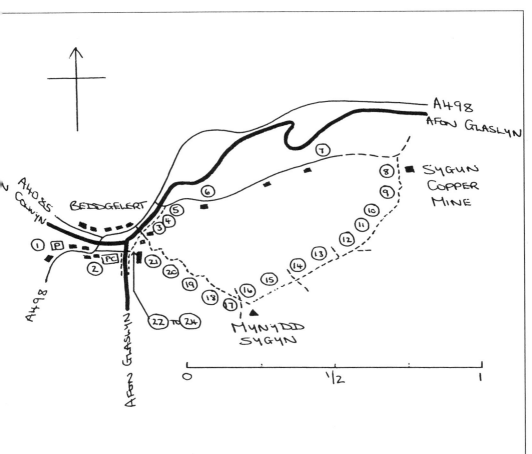

☺ After a short way you should come to a little water wheel which is part of a copper mine, where copper ore (copper in stone) was mined and loaded into those rusting trucks and brought out of the mine. Copper is a type of metal, which is often used for making water and gas pipes, statues and even roofing buildings.

Sygun Copper Mine is open daily throughout the year. Special effects are used to recreate the working atmosphere in the mine. Dogs are allowed in at the owner's discretion.

Pushchairs: those with pushchairs should now return the same way to the Starting Point.

8.   **Bear right directly before the waterwheel and follow the path leading uphill.**

☺ There are many rabbits in this area. See if you can spot them running for cover as you approach.

When the copper mine is open you can make a detour through the gate for refreshments or to visit the gift shop.

9.   **Follow the stony path uphill, going through the gate barring the track (not the gate into the grounds of the copper mine, which you should pass on your left) and continue ahead.**

☺ Here there are many more of the bushes with the large, oval leaves. Can you remember what they are called?

10. **After a short but steady climb the path veers to the right. Follow this uphill.**

☺ On the bend in the path there is a bench, which is a nice place to stop to catch your breath, and there are good views over the valley below. Can you see the stream on the opposite side of the valley tumbling down to join the river?

After a short climb you should come to another entrance to the mine. (Carefully barred by a turnstile.) It looks cold and dark inside and there is water dripping from the roof.

At this point there is another bench and viewpoint, offering further views over the valley, and there is a 3-D map showing the valley and the village.

11. **As you are looking at the mine entrance, a rocky path leads off to the right between bushes, level at first, then starting to lead uphill again.**

☺ Looking uphill you should be able to see loose stones and several small copper mines leading into the hillside. Mines can be very dangerous, so you should never go inside, unless they are open to the public, like Sygun Copper Mine below.

12. **Avoid the path which joins from the left. Keep to the main, clear stony pathway at all times, which winds and leads steadily uphill for most of the way.**

☺ Down below you should be able to see the river and the lane you walked along. Can you also see the campsite and the duck pond?

You may have to scramble over some larger rocks now, so take care, especially in wet weather, in case the rocks are slippery.

13. **Towards the top of the hill, avoid the steep narrow path off to the right. Keep to the main path. After the turning there is a signpost pointing to Sygun downhill and Beddgelert uphill. Keep right, passing the small stone shelter on the right. The path becomes more level now.**

☺ Along the top of the hills you should pass several piles of stones, which are called "cairns". It is tradition to put a stone on the top of a cairn when you pass.

14. **At the crossroads of paths head straight across. The path leads slightly uphill again and the valley should be below on your right.**

☺ Down on your left it can seem very quiet and lonely. There is dark heather and perhaps a few sheep, but nothing else. The wind is often very strong and cold up here.

15. **There is some easy scrambling over rocky areas now. The path sometimes splits and disappears altogether, so as a general rule make sure you keep right whenever there is a choice, and follow the line of the valley below.**

☺ On a fine day there are good views in all directions. You might be able to see the River Glaslyn joining the sea near Porthmadog.

16. **The path winds around a rocky crag, then leads downhill slightly before levelling off and becoming a grassy path through heather. Other paths lead off continually, but stick with the main path, and basically keep heading straight ahead at all times.**

17. **When you come to another cairn overlooking a crossroads of footpaths, bear right, which starts to wind downhill.**

☺ The rooftops and chimneys of Beddgelert should soon come into view straight ahead. Can you see the small church with the bell on its roof? In the distance are the trees of Beddgelert Forest.

Going downhill can be even more dangerous than going uphill, so take care where you put your feet and don't be tempted to run.

18. **Keep going down, as long as the path looks suitable, towards Beddgelert, which should be in sight now for most of the way back.**

19. **The path leads down to a metal kissing gate, then bears at first to the right, then starts to lead downhill. From now on the path isn't as easy to follow. There are posts to show the way, but these aren't always easy to spot, so keep straight down towards the village by the route that you consider easiest.**

Beware of rocks that might be wet and slippery. Keep small children close at hand as a certain amount of scrambling might be necessary, depending on which route you take.

20. **When you come to a grassy area between rocks it looks like the path should be heading left, but it doesn't. Keep straight ahead and look out for the yellow arrow. Sight of the village is lost for a moment, then the path leads again through rhododendrons, after which the village is in sight again.**

21. **At another point, there is a drop ahead, so bear down to the right and pick up again the clear stony path, which now descends in wide zigzags. Keep heading down towards the white cottage. Take your time and choose the easiest routes down the larger rocks.**

Q: Near the bottom of the path a white cottage should come into view. How many chimneys does it have?

A: Like the other white cottage, this one also has two.

22. **The path drops down through more rhododendrons. Go through the gate at the bottom and follow the driveway past the white cottage, leading downhill.**

☺ This white cottage was the home of Alfred Bestall, the author and illustrator of Rupert the Bear, which you may (or may not) have heard of. He was a popular cartoon character many years ago.

23. **Continue straight ahead to the river. Bear left before the bridge and return along the riverside path. After you have passed the cottages turn round and look up, and you should see the high craggy fell which you have just climbed down.**

24. **Continue to the pedestrian footbridge to return to the village.**

Beddgelert: Sygun Copper Mine Checklist

☐ A RABBIT

☐ A HORSE

☐ A SHEEP

☐ A DUCK

☐ THE SEA

☐ A WHITE COTTAGE

☐ A BRIDGE

☐ IVY GROWING ON A TREE

☐ A WATERWHEEL

☐ A WHITE STONE

☐ SOMEONE WITH A RUCKSACK

☐ SOMEONE WITH A WALKING STICK

Beddgelert: Aberglaslyn

This is a much-photographed beauty spot – and with good reason. The scenery is breath-taking, and a walk along the river offers some excellent views. The return journey, however, will not suit everyone. The footpath follows the course of an old railway line, and passes through quite a long tunnel cut through the hillside. To some this is an exciting adventure, to others a nightmare. A torch would be a very handy piece of equipment to take along but is not essential. I might add that the tunnel is quite safe and usually has a steady stream of walkers passing through it, which helps to make it less frightening. If any children (or adults for that matter) can't face it, then return to the starting point the same way along the river.

Starting Point: The car park near Nantmoor, off the A4085. (SH597462). From Beddgelert follow the main road south, towards Porthmadog. After 1½ miles bear left across the bridge towards Nantmoor. The car park is a short way on the left. This can easily be reached by foot, by following the riverside path from Beddgelert, along the course of the old railway.

By Bus: Services to Beddgelert village from Caernarfon. Services from Porthmadog: ask for Aberglaslyn.

Car Parking: At Starting Point.

Distance: 1 Mile.

Terrain: Moderate. Woodland paths, rocky in places. Some clambering necessary.

Maps: Os Landranger 115, Os Outdoor Leisure 17

Public Toilets: In The Car Park.

Refreshments: Only in Beddgelert village.

---

1.   From the car park head to the information shelter and toilets at the back of the car park. Just before the shelter go through the gate on the left, bearing to the left over the stone stile signed for "Pont Aberglaslyn". Follow the path and steps leading uphill

☺   The path is signed for "Pont Aberglaslyn". "Pont" is Welsh for bridge. "Aber" is Welsh for a pass, which is a gap between mountains, and

The Aberglaslyn Pass

"Glaslyn" is the name of the river. So in English, the sign would read: Glaslyn Pass Bridge.

2. At the top follow the path around to the left.

☺ On your right there should be a stony hillside covered with trees, mainly oaks. See if you can see any acorns on the ground. There should be plenty in the autumn. Keep a look out for squirrels, who might be looking for acorns to eat.

3. Go through the gate into the woods and follow the stony path ahead.

Q: Down on the left you might be able to see the roof of an old cottage. Can you see how many chimneys it has?

A: There are two.

4. Keep to the main path. Below you might be able to see the road between the trees. The path runs more or less parallel with the road as far as the bridge. Keep to the lower path at all times, avoiding all paths leading off uphill.

☺ There are usually lots of birds in the woods. Sparrows, blackbirds, magpies and robins to name but a few.

Q: Which of these birds is famous for its "red breast"?
A: The robin.

Q: And which of the birds is black and white?
A: The magpie.

☺ There are occasional rhododendron bushes in the woods, which have clusters of lilac flowers in the spring and summer. In the shady areas there is moss growing on the stones. Moss likes moist places where there is little sunlight, so thick woods like these are ideal. Very soon you should be able to hear the sound of rushing water from ahead.

5. Follow the steps down towards the bridge.

A kissing gate on the left allows access to the road and bridge, but if you go onto the road beware of traffic, especially as the road is not very wide, and take care of small children if you go to look over the bridge, as there is quite a drop!

6. At the bottom of the steps, bear right along the riverside path, so the river should be over on your left. (The path is somewhat fragmented, weaving its way around trees and rocks, and splitting several times. Basically just keep heading upstream by the easiest route.)

☺ This is Aberglaslyn, or the Glaslyn Pass. As you can see, there are high crags on either side of the river, with trees and bushes growing on the slopes, making it a very attractive place, very popular with walkers and tourists who come and take photographs of the river from the bridge. Down below, there are rapids, where the river runs over rocks and stones on its journey towards the sea.

Take care scrambling over rocks, especially in wet weather, when they might be slippery.

7. The path undulates fairly frequently, but is not strenuous. After some way it drops to almost river level, where a bridge crosses over a gully and the path has been worked in places to make going easier.

☺ There should now be a steep cliff up on your right with trees, ferns, heather and rhododendrons growing from it and hanging over the water. Also look out for a dark tunnel leading into the cliff. This was an old mine where metals such as copper and lead were mined. It is very dark

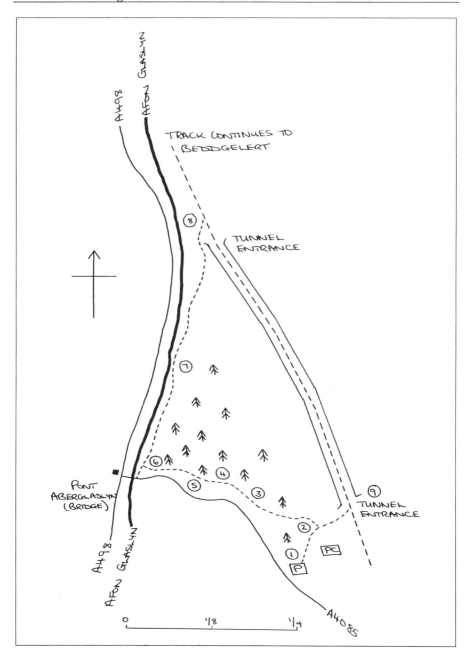

inside and very wet, with water dripping down through the rock. There are many mines like this in the area. Never go inside any mine or cave as many are unsafe or might lead for miles underground. They are not safe places to play.

8.   **After some way the path begins to climb slightly uphill, away from the river. Scramble up the stones which have been arranged into a rough set of steps, and bear right at the top onto the disused railway line. (Alternatively, bear left and follow the path straight ahead into Beddgelert.)**

☺   This path was once a railway, the Welsh Highland Railway, which ran right through the mountains. It has not been in use for a long time, and the tracks have now been taken away. It is now a popular place to walk, and you will probably pass many people who have come to enjoy the scenery.

Ahead of you is a tunnel which was cut through the rock of the hillside, which the trains would pass through. It is dark inside and there may be the odd drip of water from the ceiling, but the tunnel is quite safe, and after a short way, you should be able to see a circle of daylight at the other end.

8.   **Follow the path through the tunnel, as calmly as possible!**

Escape route: If the tunnel looks too daunting, return along the riverside, climb the steps and follow the path through the woods to the car park.

At the other end of the tunnel . . .

☺   That was probably the longest tunnel you've ever walked through. It might have been a bit scary, but also quite exciting. It is only a short way now back to the car park.

9.   **From the mouth of the tunnel, bear right and go through the wooden gate. Keep left and follow the path back down to the car park.**

Aberglaslyn checklist

- [ ] A ROCK WITH MOSS ON IT
- [ ] AN ACORN
- [ ] A TREE WITH IVY ON IT
- [ ] A STONE BRIDGE
- [ ] A SQUIRREL
- [ ] A WOODEN BENCH
- [ ] A BLACKBIRD
- [ ] A SHEEP
- [ ] A NETTLE
- [ ] A WOODEN GATE
- [ ] A METAL GATE
- [ ] A WHITE HOUSE

Walks around Betws-y-Coed

Betws-y-Coed has been a popular tourist centre since Victorian times. Situated ten miles east of Snowdon on the A4086, it couldn't really have a better location: in the heart of the Gwydir Forest. It has everything, spectacular scenery, plenty of tourist amenities, but it does get busy in the high summer.

Attractions include the renowned Swallow Falls, the railway museum (including a miniature children's railway and buffet carriage), forest and riverside walks and plenty of gift shops.

Looking down on Betws-y-Coed

Betws-y-Coed:
Afon Conwy riverside walk

A short and easy riverside walk, offering some good views of the wooded slopes that surround Betws-y-Coed. Taking in the train museum and TIC, this is a good walk for those times when the weather is fairly poor.

Starting Point: Outside Betws-y-Coed railway station. (SH795565). Well signed from the village.

By Rail: Betws-y-Coed station, on the Conwy Valley line.

Car Parking: There is a car park next to the toilets, opposite the station, and various other car parks around the village, all well-signed and suitably located.

Distance: 1½ miles

Terrain: Totally flat, footpaths and pavements mainly.

Maps:OS Landranger 115, OS Outdoor Leisure 17

Public Toilets: On the edge of the playing fields, close to the start of the walk, passed en route.

Refreshments: Various places in the village

---

1. **From the front of the railway station (with your back to the platform) bear left and follow the road towards the main road, passing the toilets on the right, overlooking the playing fields.**

2. **Bear left onto the main road and follow the pavement. Take the next left turning, signed for the golf course. There is a pavement on the right.**

☺   This is Old Church Road, and as you might guess, it leads to an old church. Notice it crosses over the railway line. As the road bears around to the left, you can see the river down on the right over the wall. This is the afon/river Conwy, which joins the sea near Conwy, where there is a castle.

The first building on the right, made of stone, is the Old Courthouse, where criminals would have their trials. It is now a hotel.

There is a public footpath sign on the right pointing down to a suspension bridge over the afon Conwy. It is worth having a look at this, but return the same way, as the path leads only to the main road.

3.   **Continue to the church. Follow the footpath sign into the church-yard, or go through the lychgate and bear right through the grave-yard, passing the church on your left. (For the railway museum follow the lane around the church, and you will come to the en-trance on the left.)**

☺   This is Saint Michael's Church, which is hundreds of years old. There is a sign near the gate which says: "Parents, do not let children climb on the graves and monuments."

There are several old yew trees around the graveyard. They have dark green needles instead of flat leaves, and some of them may have red berries. At one time the wood of yew trees was used for making coffins. People also used to believe that they had the power to keep away evil spirits.

☺   Some of the gravestones around the little church are very old. Many of them have moss and ivy growing on them. See which is the oldest you can find.

4.   **Leave the graveyard via the short steps and keep ahead along the lane. Keep a look out for any traffic.**

☺   There is now a caravan site on your left, and the river on your right, which is fairly wide and shallow at this point. Perhaps there are ducks on the water.

5.   **Keep right with the footpath, following the river.**

Q: There are many trees overhanging the path and the river, including oaks. Do you know what the "fruit" on an oak tree is called?

A: An acorn. In the autumn you will probably see lots of them on the ground. If they land in soil they will grow into a young tree.

6.   **Go through the kissing gate, keep straight ahead along the river-side path.**

☺   There is now a golf course on the left. Perhaps there are people playing at the moment. The stick they use to hit the balls is called a "club".

The river is very wide at this point, and there are islands in the middle, with trees and reeds growing on them.

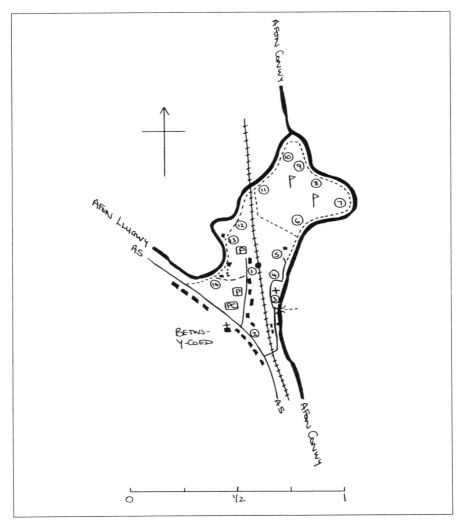

7. **There are occasional signs to point the way, but basically keep with the river.**

☺ There are good views of the forest trees on the surrounding slopes from here. In autumn they are especially colourful.

There is access to the pebbled "beach" in places.

8.   Go up the steps and keep right.

9.   Go through another kissing gate. Follow the clear path ahead.

☺ Once you've gone through the second gate there is a bench, which is a nice place to stop for a rest. Here two rivers meet, the afon Llugwy (from the left) joins the afon Conwy, and carries on along the Conwy Valley towards the sea. All rivers join the sea in the end.

10. Go through a further kissing gate. Keep left. Pass the five bar gate along the stony path. Follow the river with the golf course on your left.

☺ There are many trees along the river, including holly, which has dark, prickly leaves and red berries in the winter. It is often used as a decoration at Christmas.

Ahead you should be able to see a railway bridge. You may hear or see trains crossing over it. Perhaps you arrived here by train.

11. Continue under the bridge.

☺ In the autumn, when the trees are losing their leaves, see how many different types of leaf you can find on the ground. There are many different colours and shapes.

12. The path starts to bear away from the river, now fenced on both sides.

Q: You should pass the back of a stone house on the right. How many chimneys does it have?
A: Two.

13. Keep straight ahead, passing Royal Oak Farm Cottage on the left. Go through the gate at the end of the drive and bear left.

On the left is the entrance to the Royal Oak Stables Visitor Centre in the courtyard, well worth a visit to learn what is on offer in the area.

☺ Across the playing fields, you should be able to see the church in the centre of the village. The village is called Betws-y-coed, which means "the church in the forest".

14. Continue ahead to the station/Starting Point.

The railway museum and miniature trains at Betws-y-Coed

Afon Conwy Checklist

☐ A RAILWAY CARRIAGE

☐ A TRAIN

☐ A METAL BRIDGE

☐ A STONE BRIDGE

☐ A GRAVESTONE

☐ A CHURCH TOWER

☐ A BELL

☐ A DOG

☐ A BLACK BIRD

☐ A FLAG

☐ A BUSH WITH PRICKLES

☐ A YELLOW FLOWER

Betws-y-Coed: Miners Bridge

A moderately easy walk, along a riverside path on the way there, to the well-known "Miners Bridge" across the afon Llugwy. The river at the furthest point cuts a deep gorge through the rock and is very impressive all year round.

Starting Point: Pont-y-pair (bridge) at the north-west end of the village (SH792567), on the B5106.

By Rail: Betws-y-Coed station on the Conwy Valley line.

Car Parking: Car park at Pont-y-pair or any of the other car parks in the village, which are all only a short walk away.

Distance: 2 miles.

Terrain: Riverside paths, rocky in places, possibly muddy after heavy rain. Keep small children under control in the rocky areas. The return journey is along a quiet forest roadway.

Maps: OS Landranger 115, OS Outdoor Leisure 17.

Public Toilets: Next to the car park at the Starting Point.

Refreshments: Various places in the village.

---

1. **From the top of the bridge, overlooking the river. Cross the bridge, leading away from the main part of the village and the main road (A5). Bear left immediately after the bridge.**

☺   As you are turning left, notice on the corner a post box set into the wall. Can you see the letters E VII R on the front? This means that the post box was made when King Edward the Seventh was on the throne. The first letter on a post box is always the first letter of the king or queen's name, the R is for "Rex" or "Regina" which is Latin for king or queen.

Q: Since post boxes were first made there have only been two queens on the throne. Do you know their names?

A: Victoria and Elizabeth II.

Q: Look out also for the old slate signs on the wall. One of them points to Conway (this is the English spelling, with an "a", which is now no longer used.) How far is Conway from here?

A: 15 miles. Trefriw is 4½ miles away.

The Afon Llugwy from the Miners Bridge

On the right after the shop is a small car park and toilet block.

2. Bear left onto the rock plateau overlooking the bridge. Take care of young children near the water's edge.

Q: The bridge is called Pont-y-pair. Pont is the Welsh word meaning bridge. How many arches can you count?

A: There are five altogether, of different sizes.

On the rock plateau is the "rock cannon" which was fired on special occasions; basically holes were drilled in the stone which were then filled with gunpowder. There is a plaque about this close by and also a board with a map and information on it. Along the riverside there are occasional benches and picnic tables.

3. Follow the riverside path, so the water is on your left and you are heading upstream.

☺ This is the afon Llugwy. afon is the Welsh word meaning river. The water is very clear and shallow, and you should be able to see the stones on the bottom.

The path passes through an area of woodland where there are many different types of tree, some of them have ivy growing up their trunks. Ivy is a climbing plant and has tiny suckers to help it climb. Some of the trees are oaks, so look for acorns on the ground in autumn. Acorns are the seeds of the oak tree.

Q: Some of the bushes in the forest have prickly, dark green leaves. What are they called?

A. Holly.

4. Towards the end of the woods there is rocky crag. Keep this on your right, close to the river. The path leads to a ladder stile at the back of the crag. Climb over and follow the clear path leading alongside the river.

☺ The path now crosses an open grassy field where there might be sheep or cows. See if you can see any sheep wool on the ground.

5. Cross the wooden footbridge over the small stream and continue ahead.

☺ There are views on both sides of the forest that surrounds the village. Most of the trees are "conifers", which have dark needles instead of flat leaves. Many conifers are "evergreen" which means they do not lose their colour in the autumn, but not all conifers are, as you will see if it happens to be autumn. Some of the forest trees will be a yellow or brown colour.

6. You should come to another ladder stile at the end of the field. Cross over. The path starts to lead slightly uphill through trees. It can be muddy at this point after heavy rain, but it is easy enough to pick your way using the stones. Basically, keep following the

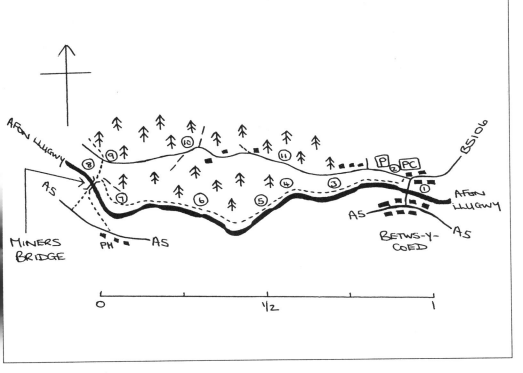

river (Take care with younger children on the rocks. There is a drop down to the river in places.)

7.   The path starts to climb above the river, and there is a fence on the left. At the top is the Miners Bridge over the river.

☺   This is the Miners Bridge, which was originally built so that miners could cross over to reach mines in the forest over the river. The mines are all closed now and overgrown.

If you cross the bridge notice the sign saying "pergyl" which is the Welsh word meaning "danger". Take care as the bridge can be slippery, so hold on tightly to the handrail.

8.   If you have crossed the bridge return to the same side of the river and continue straight upwards through the trees. (There is a sign on one of the trees pointing the way.) There is a rough path, but if you lose it keep straight ahead, uphill.

☺ The path climbs quite steeply through tall conifers. Can you remember what that means? Conifers have their seeds in cones, so see if you can find any on the ground.

9.   When you come to the forest roadway turn right.

☺ This is a working forest. The trees are grown for their wood, so you may see that parts have been cut down. If you see any logs, try and count how many rings there are on the round ends. This should tell you how old the tree was. There should be one ring for every year.

In other places new trees might have been planted. It takes twenty to thirty years for these trees to grow to the right height. They are chosen for their wood because they grow tall and straight and can easily be sawn into planks. How many things can you think of that are made of wood?

10. Avoid the trackway leading to the right, back towards the river, and the one to the left leading higher into the forest. Keep with the roadway.

☺ In places there are views down to the right over the fields to the river. Can you see the path you walked along earlier? Perhaps there are people walking along it now.

You should pass a stone house with several tall chimneys, after which the road climbs slightly, then it is downhill all the way.

11. Keep to the roadway, leading downhill, avoiding all trackways and footpaths to either side.

☺ Soon you come to the first of the houses on the left, which is where the village begins. It is only a short way further to the end of the walk.

Miners Bridge Checklist

☐ A DOG

☐ A SHEEP

☐ A COW

☐ A STONE BRIDGE

☐ A WOODEN BRIDGE

☐ A TREE WITH BERRIES

☐ A TREE WITH PRICKLES

☐ SOMEONE WITH A RUCKSACK

☐ SOMEONE WITH A WALKING STICK

☐ A FIR CONE

☐ AN ACORN

☐ A BIRD'S FEATHER

Betws-y-Coed: Llyn Elsi

Quite a strenuous walk to a secluded beauty spot within the Gwyddyr Forest, which never gets very busy, because it is quite a climb to get there and there is no road running anywhere near it. Well worth the uphill hike.

Starting Point: The Church, (SH794564) Betws-y-Coed village. Opposite the playing fields.

Distance: 3 miles.

By Bus: Services from Llandudno, Blaenau and Llanberis.

Car Parking: Several well-signed car parks in the village centre.

Terrain: A climb along Forest trackways and craggy footpaths on the way to Llyn Elsi, and downhill all the way back.

Maps: OS Outdoor Leisure 16, OS Landranger 115

Public Toilets: In the village, next to the sports field. Well signed.

Refreshments: Various places in the village.

---

1. **Take one of the roads that leads behind the church, and follow the wide stony trackway that leads directly uphill into the forest, signed for Llyn Elsi. Keep to the main trackway.**

☺ This path is quite steep in places, but if you take it slowly and stop whenever you need to, it shouldn't be such hard work. If you walk at a speed that is comfortable for you, walking uphill can be almost as easy as walking on the flat. (I only said *almost!*)

There are many different types of tree in the forest, but they are mainly oaks at this point. The forest is very colourful in the autumn when many of the leaves change colour. Between the trees there are prickly blackberries and a type of fern called bracken, which also changes colour in the autumn, going from green to brown or yellow.

Some of the trees have ivy growing on them, which is a climbing plant which can hook onto the rough bark of the tree with its tiny suckers. It can also be found climbing on walls, rocks and spreading across the ground like a green carpet.

There may be many birds in the forest, including sparrows, blackbirds, crows and magpies. In the winter, when the trees are bare, look for nests high up amongst the branches, made out of twigs and dried leaves, which the male and female birds gather, carrying each piece back in their beaks.

Soon, on the left, look out for some stone ruins, which would probably once have been a small cottage or farm building. The roof has long since fallen in and there are plants growing in what would have been the rooms. Never play on or near ruins like this, because they can be very dangerous.

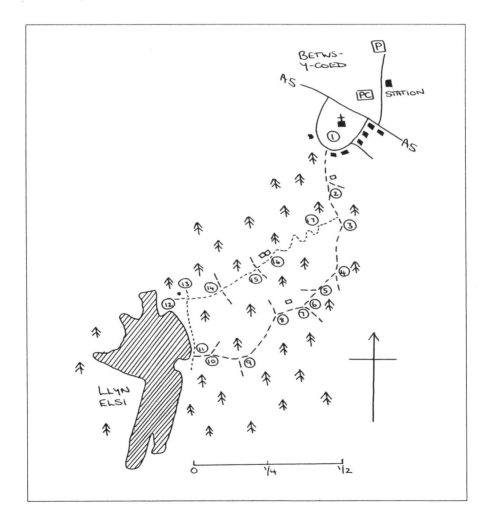

2. **Avoid the grassy path off to the left towards the stone ruin. Continue uphill along the main path, which soon bears sharply around to the right.**

☺ You might be able to hear a waterfall downhill on your left and soon there is a small stream on your right along the side of the track, with ferns and other water-loving plants growing along it, and moss growing on the rocks. Moss is a bit like a sponge. It soaks up moisture when it is wet and dries out when there is no water around, and can seem quite dry and dead, but as soon as it rains it comes back to life again.

Take care as there is a drop to the left of the track.

You should pass by a wooden bench, which is a handy place to stop and have a rest before you carry on up the hill.

3. **Continue straight ahead after the bench, again signed for Llyn Elsi.**

☺ Most of the trees in the forest so far have had large, flat leaves, like oaks and sycamores, but now there are trees along the trackway which have dark "needles" instead of leaves. These are called "conifers", and they carry their seeds in cones which fall from the tree. Look on the ground and see if you can find any cones. There are many different types of conifer, and they all have different cones, some very small, and some quite large. See how many different types of cone you can find.

This is a working forest, which means that some of the trees are cut down every year for their wood. Conifers are grown for their wood because they grow tall and straight, and they are quite fast growing compared to other types of tree, though it takes twenty or thirty years before a tree is ready to be cut down, or "felled" as it is called, so all these trees around you will be several times older than you are.

You might see men at work "felling" the trees. There should be yellow signs to warn you that they are at work. They wear "hard hats" to protect their heads from falling trees and branches.

4. **At the junction keep right, now following the blue and white topped posts, still leading uphill, I'm afraid. (Do not go off to the left here, as there are steep drops, so don't let children wander alone through the trees.)**

☺ Look for the rocky cliff on the right, where you can see the roots of trees sticking out, in search of water. The tree eats and drinks through its roots, getting nourishment from the soil.

There should be views to the left between the trees over the Conwy Val-

Llyn Elsi

ley below. There are more forests on the far side of the valley, some of which might recently have been felled. Once an area has been cleared of trees it is replanted with young trees, or "saplings".

5.   Avoid all turnings into the forest and stick with the main trackway, still following the blue and white posts.

☺ Below on the right you might be able to see crumbling stone walls, which at one time would have separated fields, long before all the trees were planted. This type of wall is called a "drystone" wall, because it is made of dry stones carefully balanced, and has no cement to hold the stones together. They are usually so well made that they last for hundreds of years.

6.   After a short way you should come to a junction where the blue and white posts split. Here bear right and follow the white posts.

☺ The trees are now mainly tall conifers, with their dark needles and straight trunks. Keep a look out still for different types of fir cones. In dry weather the wooden "petals" on a fir cone are open, like a flower, and in wet weather they are tightly closed.

Look out also for squirrels, who eat the seeds within the cones. There are two types of squirrel: red and grey. The greys are by far the most common, and reds are very rare. Grey squirrels are better at surviving and when short of food, will often raid bird tables and litter bins. They eat many different types of seeds, nuts and young shoots.

7.   At the T-junction bear right, still following the white topped posts.

Q: Hundreds of different types of insects live in the forest, including bees, wasps, butterflies, ants, ladybirds and other beetles. How many legs does an insect have?

A: Insects have six legs, so spiders, which have eight legs, aren't actually a member of the insect family, though there are still plenty of them in the forest!

☺ Look out for some more ruins almost hidden in the undergrowth. You should be able to see the chimneys rising above all the greenery.

8.   At the next junction bear left, still with the white topped posts.

☺ In wet weather there may be small streams running along the side of the path. In warm weather these will dry up altogether. The streams run down to the rivers in the valley below, and are carried between the mountains and off to join the sea.

Notice that when the trees are close together nothing can grow on the ground underneath them, because there isn't enough light. All plants need light to grow. Where the trees are further apart sunlight can reach the forest floor and there are plants and grass.

9. **Further junction, again keep with the white topped posts, this time bearing right.**

☺ There are many plants in the forest which have berries in the late summer and autumn. You have probably already seen lots of blackberries, which are very common. Also you might have noticed prickly hawthorn bushes with their dark red berries. There are also bilberries, which are small and black, and grow close to the ground, and wild raspberries, which are like blackberries, only red. Although some wild berries are safe to eat, many are not, and can be quite poisonous, so never pick or eat wild berries unless an adult says it is safe.

10. **At the next junction bear left.**

☺ This is also a cycle route, so you might see people on mountain bikes.

This is the last part of the journey and, after a short way the lake, Llyn Elsi comes into view. The Welsh word "Llyn" means "lake".

There are trees surrounding Llyn Elsi and it has many little coves and small beaches around its edges. It is used as a reservoir, which is a place where water is stored until it is needed.

11. **Look out for the path bearing off to the right above the lakeshore. Follow this as it meanders among trees and boulders, still following the white topped posts.**

☺ In the distance all around, above the treetops are the high hills and mountains of Snowdonia. They might even be covered with snow or cloud. In fact, in bad weather, you won't be able to see them at all.

12. **Follow the path as it leads over the rocks to the monument. Some scrambling might be necessary.**

☺ This is the furthest point in the walk, and it's downhill nearly all the way back.

Q: Look at the monument which tells that this reservoir was opened by the local water works, but in which year?

A: 1914

13. **At the monument, while looking at the lake, take the path which should lead off to your left, so that the lake is over on your right. This is a clear path between ferns which rises slightly and is soon completely surrounded by trees.**

☺ Notice how the trees are growing very close together now, and there are very few plants growing on the forest floor. This is because all plants need sunlight to grow and the trees here are so close that little or no light can reach the ground, so there are just dry, dead needles which have fallen from the conifers.

There might be muddy places along the path, where you will probably see some footprints, not only left by people, but also animals. See if you can see any animal prints, and can you tell which animal left them?

14. **At the forest trackway head straight across and continue along the footpath.**

☺ You will probably pass several fallen tree trunks, which have been left to rot. They might be covered with moss or growths of fungus. The soft decaying wood makes a home for hundreds of insects, which can burrow easily into the soft wood.

15. **Cross over a further forest trackway and continue ahead along a craggy footpath, leading downhill. There are again white posts from now on.**

☺ After a short way you should come to the ruins of a building on the left. There are trees growing in it and over the crumbling walls. It must have been a lonely place, high up here, far away from the village.

16. **The path now leads downhill in a series of zigzags. It is quite steep in parts, so keep hold of small children.**

☺ This next part of the path is quite steep, so you should take care where you are walking. If you are reading this while you are walking you shouldn't be! Watch where you are going! As you get lower you should be able to hear the stream below, and also traffic on the roads in the village. If you get bored just looking at your feet, try counting how many steps it takes you to reach the bottom.

17. **At the bottom cross the footbridge over the stream and continue to the forest trackway, bearing left back to the village.**

☺ This is the same trackway from the beginning of the walk. Can you recognise it? It is quite steep and you have to "keep your brakes on" which can put a strain on your legs. Going downhill isn't always easier than going uphill.

Q: As you get lower, you should be able to see the rooftops and chimneys of the village below. Here is a memory test for you. You passed the church at the beginning of the walk. Does it have a tower or a spire? And does it have a clock or a sundial?

A: It has a tower and a clock.

☺ The church should soon come into view between the trees, so you should be able to see if you were right. Once you can see the church, it should tell you that this is the end of the walk.

Llyn Elsi Checklist

☐ A FIRCONE

☐ A WOODEN BRIDGE

☐ A SLATE MONUMENT

☐ A LOG

☐ A MOUNTAIN STREAM

☐ A CONIFER/EVERGREEN TREE

☐ A PERSON WITH A RUCKSACK

☐ A SQUIRREL

☐ RED BERRIES IN AUTUMN/WHITE FLOWERS IN SUMMER

☐ IVY ON A TREE TRUNK

☐ MOSS GROWING ON A ROCK

Walks around Conwy

Conwy is the northern gateway to Snowdonia, reached off the A55. This is a popular walled town on the afon Conwy. It has an attractive quayside and is famous for its castle. There are all the usual seaside amenities, including boat trips, gift shops and a bit of sand. For proper beaches you need to follow the riverside path towards the sea. Conwy is also home to the "Smallest House in Britain", which as its name suggests, is quite small.

Conwy: harbour, castle and woodland

Conwy: Quayside & Town

A very short walk which serves as an introduction to Conwy, taking in the town, the quay, woodland and castle walls (under them, not on them). Something to see whatever the weather, and you're never too far away from the starting point.

Starting Point: The Quayside, Conwy (SH783776). Well-signed, no matter how you get into town.

By Rail: Conwy station (request stop only). The nearest station is Llandudno junction, just a short walk to the town centre.

Car Parking: Various car parks, well signed.

Distance: Just over a mile.

Maps: OS Landranger 115, OS Outdoor Leisure 17.

Public Toilets: At the castle and on the quayside, both well signed. Also in the gardens towards the end of the route.

Refreshments: Various cafés, pubs and restaurants.

Pushchairs: The first half of the route along the quayside walkway is ideal for pushchairs. At the woods return the same way to the town.

---

1. **Head along the quayside, so that the water is on your right.**

☺ This is the River Conwy, which joins the sea close by. This part of the river is "tidal", which means the sea comes this far up it at high tide. This stone area you are walking along is called a "quay" or "quayside" and is where boats would come to load and unload. Today it is used mainly for pleasure boats. Watch carefully where you are walking, because there might be ropes which you could trip over!

There are toilets on the left, built into the old town walls.

Escape route: To cut the route drastically short, bear left and go through the archway between the toilets and the pub. Continue to the main road and bear left, then follow Direction 14.)

2. **Continue along the quayside.**

The "Conwy Frigate" at the quayside

Q: There is a pub on the quayside named after a well-known city in northern England. What is it called?

A: The "Liverpool Arms".

☺   On the left look out for "the smallest house in Britain" which is a tiny cottage, more like a cupboard than a house. When it is open there is usually a lady standing outside in traditional Welsh costume, including a black hat. Can you spot her?

The "Smallest House" is open to the public. Also from the quayside there are various boat trips available up and down the river and out to sea.

☺   Keep a look out for cottages with butterflies on them. Not real butterflies of course, but large models which are made in Wales. These are sold in gift shops. Can you think of five things you might buy as a gift from the seaside?

3.   **Go through the archway in the town walls and follow the lane past "Boat House" on the left, at which point there is a junction. Here bear right, leading downhill, signed as the North Wales Path.**

Q: You should pass two houses with names connected with the sea. Can you spot them?

A: "Boat House" and "Shore Cottage". Both are on the left, and both have name plaques, so they are quite easy to see.

4.   **The path leads you along the estuary of the river.**

☺   This is the mouth or "estuary" of the River Conwy, near where it joins the sea. As you can see it is very popular for boating, and there will be boats anchored in rows across the river, and some boats pulled up on the shingle beach. Many of the boats are given women's' names. See if you can spot any.

Q: There are often ducks, geese and swans on the beach. Do you know what a young swan is called?

A: A cygnet.

☺   There are good views back towards the castle and quay. In the other direction, in the distance, the sea should come into view. There is a road tunnel passing underneath the river not far from here. Perhaps you have been through it. It saves traffic having to drive all the way to the bridge near the castle, and saves a lot of vehicles having to pass through the busy town. A lot of traffic which forms a traffic jam is called "congestion". This happens because there are too many cars on the roads.

5. Go through the open gateway in the high wall on the left (just before you reach the school playing field.) Follow the path (signed occasionally with arrows) straight ahead, leading uphill into the woods.

Q: There are many mixed trees in the woods, including beech, oak, hawthorn and sycamore. Which of these trees has thorns?

A: Hawthorn. It also has white or pink blossom in the spring and small red berries in the winter, which get eaten by birds and other small animals that live in the woods. They are not suitable for people to eat though, even though they might be a nice bright colour. Never touch any wild berries or mushrooms, as some are very poisonous and can make you ill.

6. At the junction bear left following the arrow, up a fairly steep hill between holly bushes. Only a short climb.

☺   There are many holly bushes on either side of the path now, as you climb up the hill. As you will know, holly has prickly leaves, and sometimes red berries in the autumn. It doesn't lose its leaves in the winter, so it is often used for Christmas decorations. You may have heard the Christmas Carol "The Holly and the Ivy". Ivy is another plant which does not lose its leaves in the winter.

7. At the clear cross roads of footpaths continue straight ahead.

☺   After a short way you should pass the stump of a large tree which was cut down, probably because it had become unsafe. You might be able to see parts of its trunk in the undergrowth, which might have fungus or moss growing on them. Old wood like this makes an ideal home for hundreds of tiny insects, which can burrow easily into the soft, dead wood.

Q: How many legs do insects have?

A: Six.

8. Various paths lead off, but continue straight ahead, which soon begins to wind downhill.

☺   Most of the bushes along the path are "rhododendrons" which have large, oval leaves. In the summer they have large clusters of lilac flowers which attract many insects.

9. Keep with the main path, which should take you down a set of

steps. At the bottom bear left. There should be a car park on your right. Cross over the car park driveway and continue ahead towards the white house, which is now a council building. Follow the driveway in front of the building.

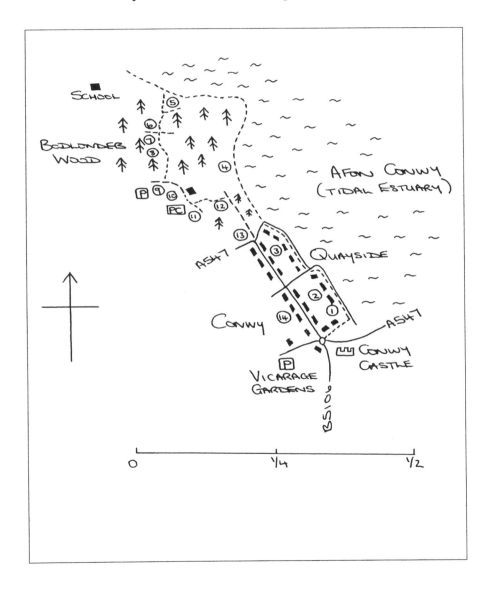

☺ In front of the house there is a war memorial on the right, in memory of people who died in the First and Second World Wars. There are often "wreaths" of red flowers around it. A wreath is a circle of flowers, often sent to funerals. The red flowers are poppies.

10. **Pass the front of the house after which a path leads in both directions around the lawn. Follow the path to the right, which will take you to the public toilets.**

Q: Outside the toilets there is a signpost in Welsh and English. What is the Welsh word for "castle"?

A: Almost the same, "Castell".

11. **At the signpost bear left, signed for The Marine Walk. The path winds around the lawn and starts to lead slightly downhill through the trees.**

Alternatively, at the toilets continue straight ahead following the sign for the castle. This will take you past a children's playground. Continue ahead to the park gates and bear left along the road, following it around to the right which will take you back into the centre of the town.

12. **The path leads downhill to a driveway. Bear right. This is a quiet driveway, but stay alert in case of any vehicles.**

☺ There are occasional views between the trees on the left over the river and boats. Perhaps there are some boats sailing out to sea. Look out for the benches, which are a nice place to stop for a rest or picnic.

13. **Go through the large gateway at the end of the drive and continue ahead, following the road. Pass under the arches in the town walls and follow the main street.**

Alternatively, bear left downhill and retrace your steps around to the right, back to the quayside and return to the town centre that way.

☺ This is Castle Street, and not surprisingly it leads to the castle. It is one of the main streets in the town, and one of the busiest. Look out for Swan Cottage on the left which has a sign on the wall, showing a picture of a swan swimming in the river in front of the castle.

Q: Look out for a chip shop named after a boat. Can you spot it?
A: "The Galleon".

Q: Look out for the "Blue Bell Inn" on the left, with a picture of a bell on the sign. What is the date underneath the bell?
A: 1935.

14. **At the end of the shops, in the shadow of the castle, bear left and follow the path through the archway in the town walls, back to the quayside/Starting Point.**

There are further public toilets across the roundabout close to the new castle entrance.

☺ Notice there is a wishing well on a small area of grass before you go under the arch and back to the quay. This is now the end of the walk.

Conwy Quayside Checklist

☐ A CASTLE

☐ A BOAT WITH SAILS

☐ A BOAT WITHOUT SAILS

☐ A SWAN

☐ A DUCK

☐ A PINK FLOWER (IN SPRING)

☐ AN ACORN (IN AUTUMN)

☐ A SEAGULL

☐ A DOG

☐ A SQUIRREL

☐ A RED CAR

☐ A FLAG

Conwy: above the Conwy Valley

A more strenuous walk offering views over the town, castle and the Conwy Valley. A quiet route and a good introduction to uphill walking.

Starting Point: Morfa Bach car park, off Llanrwst Road, (B5106) Conwy (SH782773). From the small roundabout in front of the castle head under the arch and follow the signs for the car park, which is on the right.

By Rail: Llandudno Junction station, just a short walk away.

Car Parking: At Starting Point.

Distance: 2½ miles.

Terrain: Footpaths and quiet lanes, some uphill stretches, though the worst part is the initial climb.

Maps: OS Landranger 115. OS Outdoor Leisure 17.

Public Toilets: In the car park.

Refreshments: Available in the car park, or various places in the town centre.

---

1.   **From the car park bear left along the road. Cross carefully and take the signed footpath off to the right. Keep straight uphill towards the woods.**

☺   (At the top of the field.) Turn around and look back over the town. There is a good view of the castle and the bridges that cross the River Conwy. There are two tunnels going into the railway bridge. You might be lucky enough to see a train going into the tunnel, or coming out.

There are often pigeons and seagulls perched on the top of castle walls. The tall round towers are called "turrets". Can you count how many turrets there are?

2.   **Climb the ladder stile and follow the path leading around to the right, around the edge of the woods.**

☺   The path climbs steadily, but it isn't too steep. There are many different flowers along the path and at the edge of the woods. In the spring there are bluebells everywhere. In the woods there are many different types of tree, including beech and oak, which are popular with squirrels, because they both have a "fruit" in the autumn, which squirrels can eat.

The fruit of the beech tree is called a "beechnut". The fruit of the oak tree is an acorn, which you have probably seen many times.

Some of the bushes along the path are prickly, like hawthorn and holly, which both have red berries in the autumn. Also look out for prickly "gorse", which has yellow flowers in the summer, which can last for most of the year.

3. **Keep to the main path, with the fenced woodlands on your left. At the top climb the stile and continue straight ahead.**

☺ You should pass several troughs full of water, which are for cows to drink from. A cow can drink a lot of water in a day, so there needs to be plenty for them. These troughs are fitted with a special type of tap, which fills up automatically as the water starts to get low.

4. **Go through the kissing gate and continue ahead to the signpost. Here bear right, cross the ladder stile and continue ahead.**

☺ Looking over to your right there are further views over the castle, town walls and the river estuary all the way to the open sea, where there might be boats sailing up the river towards Conwy.

Q: After a short way there are hedges on both sides of the path. The hedges are made up of many different plants, including gorse, hawthorn and brambles. Do you know which of these plants have berries in the late summer and autumn?

A: The hawthorn has red berries. Brambles are very common, but you might know them better as blackberries. Although some berries you

Conwy castle from the woods

might find on your walk are safe to eat, like blackberries, some berries are very poisonous, so never eat wild berries unless a grown-up says you can, and even then it isn't a very good idea, because they might be coated with chemicals which farmers have sprayed their fields with.

5.   Straight ahead is a large mast or transmitter on the top of the hill. Follow the track as it bears slightly to the left before continuing again towards the transmitter and stone farm buildings.

Q: Look out for a weathervane on the top of one of the buildings. What do you think a weathervane is for?

A: It shows which way the wind is blowing. Can you tell which way the wind is blowing today?

6.   Go through the kissing gate and continue straight ahead, through a gateway signed as a footpath. Follow the rutted trackway passing behind the farm buildings.

☺ On the left there are open grassy fields. In the distance on the top of a hill is another transmitter. Can you see it? As you pass behind the farm look out for another weathervane with a dog on it, and chimney pots and an old bath filled with plants and flowers.

Q: How many chimneys are there on the roof of the farm house?

A: Two.

7.   At the end of the driveway bear right along the lane. (Although this is a quiet lane, please beware of any possible vehicles.)

Escape route: To cut the route in half, bear left along the lane. Avoid the footpath off to the right and continue from Direction 14.

Q: There are high grassy banks along the lane, with hedges, again made up of many different plants, such as gorse, hawthorn, ivy , nettles and oak saplings. What is a "sapling"?

A: A sapling is a young tree. See if you can see any amongst the hedges.

8.   Pass the farm driveway leading to the left and continue downhill along the lane. Take the signed footpath off to the left, going through the kissing gate and keep straight ahead, with your back to the lane. Cross the small stream and bear right, following the clear footpath leading gradually uphill beneath trees.

9.   When the path opens into the field cut straight across, bearing slightly uphill towards the outcrop of gorse. The path leads through the bushes, and is marked in places with yellow-topped

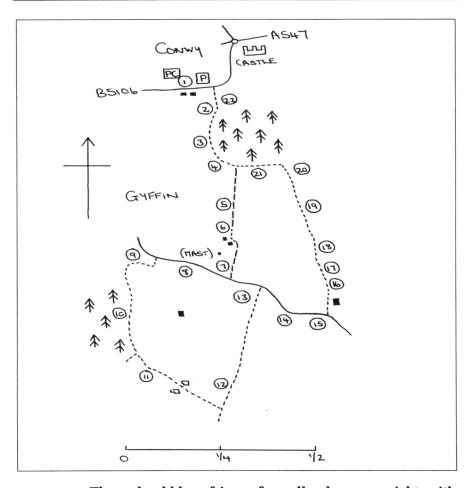

posts. There should be a fringe of woodland on your right, with the occasional tree trunk with yellow paint marks on it to reassure you of the route. Don't follow any of the sheep tracks down into the woods.

☺ There are many outcrops of prickly gorse in these fields. The thorns are very sharp, so take care not to cut yourself. Can you think of any other plants or trees which have prickles or thorns? Here are a few: roses, holly, brambles and hawthorn, but there are many others.

10. Keep with the edge of the woods and avoid any gateways leading

off. **By following the yellow posts you should come to a stile on the right. Cross over and as the arrow shows, bear diagonally left, passing another outcrop of gorse on your left.**

☺ Many of these fields will probably have cows in them. The cows might be curious, especially if they are young, and might come towards you. There is no need to be afraid of them, but if you are frightened, clap loudly and they will run away.

11. **The path leads through some low stone ruins, where there are occasional yellow painted stones and arrows marking the way. Once through the ruins keep straight ahead, passing an old barn on the right. At the end of the drystone wall bear left and keep ahead until you come to a T-junction with another clear and signed footpath. Bear left and keep straight ahead along the edge of the field.**

12. **Go through gateways and keep ahead along the edge of the fields. The path starts to lead uphill. Avoid any gateways to the right.**

Q: Can you see the white farmhouse over on the left? How many chimneys does it have?

A: Same as the last one: two.

13. **Go through the gate and bear right onto the lane.**

14. **Follow the lane downhill.**

☺ To the right of the gate look out for a metal post near the gate on the right, partly hidden in the undergrowth. You should be able to make out the word "Conway" on it. This was once a boundary mark, to show the edge of the town of Conway.

☺ You might have noticed there are two ways of spelling Conwy/Conway. The first way is the Welsh way. The second, with the "a", is the English way.

There should be views ahead over the River Conwy. You might see or hear a train on the other side, rattling along the Conwy valley. Perhaps you have been for a ride on this train.

Q: You should soon be able to see the rooftops of a farm down on your left. What is the name of the farm?

A: "Farm Yard". There should be a hanging sign at the gate showing the name.

15. **Climb the ladder stile on the left directly before the farm driveway. Continue ahead across the field, so the farm buildings are
on your right, to a further ladder stile.**

☺ There might be cows in any of the grassy fields from now on. There are
many different types of cow. For example, the common black and white
cows are called "Friesians", but there are also many different types of
brown cow. See how many different colours of cow you can see. A
group of cows together is called a "herd". A herd of cows.

16. **Climb the stile and continue ahead to a further stile.**

Q: What is a young cow called?

A: A calf.

17. **Again climb the stile and continue straight ahead to the next stile.**

☺ There might also be sheep in these fields. Most of the sheep will be
white, though there are black and brown ones occasionally. Like cows,
sheep spend most of their time eating grass. A group of sheep together
is called a "flock". A flock of sheep.

18. **Climb the stile (there should be what looks like a stone ruin on
your right surrounded by trees). Again continue straight ahead.
At present the next ladder stile has lost its wall, there is only a low
line of stones where the wall once stood. Cross over and continue
ahead to the end of the field. Here bear right until you come to the
stile close to an outcrop of gorse bushes.**

☺ Again you should be passing some of those prickly bushes called
gorse, with their strong, sweet-smelling yellow flowers, which sometimes smell a bit like coconut. There might be other flowers in the fields,
like buttercups, daisies, dandelions and clover, which attract butterflies
and other insects. If it is a fine sunny day you will probably see several of
them fluttering across the fields.

19. **Climb the stile and continue straight ahead across the small field
to the next stile.**

☺ You may now be able to see Conwy again, and in the background is
Conwy Mountain. Can you see any sheep on the sides of the mountain?
Or perhaps you can see walkers climbing to the top? The very top of a
hill or mountain is called the "summit". Have you ever climbed to the
summit of a hill?

20.   Climb the stile and bear left along the edge of the field.

☺ The field now heads slightly downhill and you might be pleased to hear there is no more walking uphill now. The area ahead might look familiar, because you walked here earlier on.

21.   At the signpost keep straight ahead, and retrace your steps along the woodland footpath.

Q: How many of the bushes in the woods have prickles?
A: Gorse, holly and blackberry.

☺ Have you seen any squirrels on your walk yet? If not, now is your chance. If you keep quiet for a minute or two they might come out of hiding in search of nuts to eat.

22.   Climb the stile and continue straight across the field. Bear left along the road, back to the car park and starting point.

Conwy Valley Checklist

☐   A BLACK COW

☐   A BROWN COW

☐   A SHEEP

☐   A TRANSMITTER

☐   A TRAIN

☐   A WHITE FLOWER (IN SPRING)

☐   AN ACORN (IN AUTUMN)

☐   A METAL GATE

☐   A WHITE BUILDING

☐   A RABBIT

Walks around The Dyfi Estuary

The Dyfi valley is very attractive, with rolling green hills and pockets of woodland, and from many places there are good views across the wide estuary of the Afon Dyfi. The river marks the southern boundary of Snowdonia.

Aberdyfi/Aberdovey is the main holiday resort of the area, where the Afon Dyfi joins the sea. Aberdyfi is surprisingly unspoilt, the sort of place that people refer to as "charming". It was once a busy port, now it is busy because of its fine beach and its tourist amenities. There is a (seasonal) ferry across the mouth of the river, and all manner of sailing and boating craft available for hire. On the promenade, there is a National Park Information Centre.

Boats on the Dyfi estuary

Dyfi Estuary: Aberdyfi (Aberdovey)

This is a fairly strenuous walk on the outward journey, but completely flat on the way back, which happens to be along the beach. Aberdyfi is an attractive little seaside town and the sandy beaches make it very popular. Don't forget your bucket and spade!

Starting Point: The sea front, Aberdyfi, anywhere in the region of the main car park, (SH613959), just off the A493.

By Bus: Scenic bus ride from Tywyn or Machynlleth.

By Rail: Aberdyfi Station. From the station follow the approach road, keeping straight ahead along the footpath as the road bears to the left, so you are following the line of the railway. This will lead you into the town.

Car Parking: Next to the Starting Point on the sea front, or any of the other local car parks, all well signed.

Distance: Just over 3½ miles.

Terrain: The outward route follows Aberdyfi's promenade for a way before bearing inland along footpaths crossing the headland. The return journey is entirely along the sandy beach.

Maps: OS Landranger 135, OS Outdoor Leisure 23.

Public Toilets: Aberdyfi, towards the end of the prom, passed en route, close to the start of the walk.

Refreshments: Various places in Aberdyfi.

---

1.   **Follow the promenade above the beach.**

☺   This is Aberdyfi, a nice little seaside town. On your left there are hotels, shops and cafés looking out to sea, all painted bright, cheerful colours. On your right is the beach and the sea. On a sunny day it is a popular place to play or paddle.

2.   **Follow the prom as it bears to the left, passing the toilets and Tourist Information Centre. At the end of the prom go through the narrow gateway onto the pavement and cross over the road towards the Dovey Inn.**

Q: The black and white building in front of you is called the Dovey Inn, and it is very old. If you look carefully you should be able to find out when it was built.

The beach at Aberdyfi

A: The date is on the front of the building. It was built in 1729.

There is a beer garden at the rear of the inn.

3.   **Bear right after the inn down Copperhill Street. Keep straight ahead and pass under the railway bridge.**

Q: The triangular sign on the railway bridge shows the height of the bridge. How high is it?

A: It says on the sign 10'0", which means ten feet and no inches.

4.   **After the bridge look out for the path off to the left with railings along it, and follow this uphill between the backs of the cottages. You should come to a wire fence on the left with the railway beyond it. Take the right turning leading further uphill between hedges and undergrowth. This opens out and becomes a rough trackway. Continue ahead.**

☺   You have already climbed quite a way uphill. Soon you should be able to see the sea over on the left.

5.   **The trackway becomes a tarmac road. Continue ahead. At the junction cross straight over, cross the ladder stile and bear left. Keep the fence on your left.**

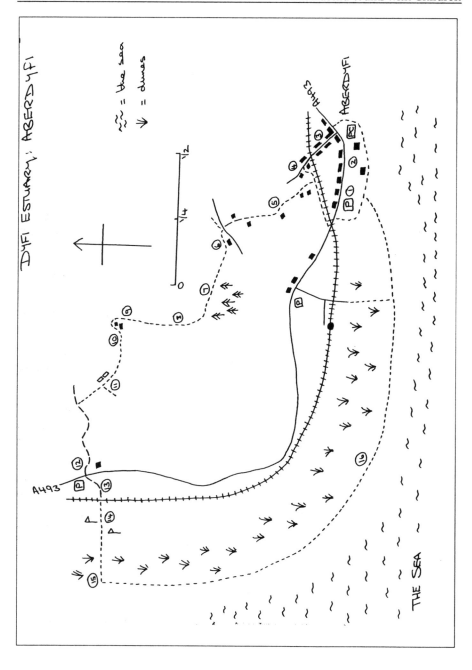

Escape route: Instead of crossing over the road bear left and follow it down-hill. Take care at the bottom as it leads to the main road. Bear left along the pavement for the town centre. Alternatively, take the turning marked for the station, pass under the railway bridge and keep straight ahead through the sand dunes which will take you onto the beach. Bear left to return to Aberdyfi.

☺ More uphill walking, I'm afraid. There are many prickly bushes along the path, which have yellow flowers in the summer. These are called "gorse". The flowers sometimes smell a bit like coconut.

As you climb higher there are views out to sea, and over the rooftops of Aberdyfi. See if you can spot: the railway line, a caravan, a boat, a red car, a dog on the beach.

6. **The path is quite clear and easy to follow, not straying very far from the fence on the left. The path levels out, then climbs quite steeply to a ladder stile. Cross over and continue ahead.**

☺ There are often sheep in these fields. See if you can spot any of their wool in the grass.

7. **Climb a further ladder stile and continue ahead, keeping with the fence on the left.**

☺ In the distance you might be able to see the ruins of some stone farm buildings, which you will later be passing. Don't worry, they aren't as far away as they look.

8. **The path passes through an area of low gorse and becomes indistinct. Just make sure you have the fence in sight on your left.**

☺ There is a farm below now. See if you can see a tractor anywhere in the fields, or hens in the farmyard.

9. **The path leads downhill to a small stream. Stride over and bear around to the left, still with the fence, passing the back of the farm. Once past the farmhouse go through the metal gate on the left, signed with a yellow arrow, and follow the trackway leading straight ahead, downhill, to a footpath sign at the bottom, pointing to the right. Follow this in a straight line, passing the tall conifer on your left, then follow the path to the left, down into the dip and across the stream via the small footbridge.**

10. **Once over the stream climb the stile and continue straight ahead, leading up the open hillside. Once up the first ridge you should**

come across a well-worn path. Follow this, which at first leads towards the sea, then begins to bear around to the right. As you
round the hillside the stone ruins should come into view ahead.

☺ Do you recognise these ruins from before, when they looked a long way
away? The roofs have fallen in and the buildings are now dangerous.
You should never play in old ruins like these.

Escape route: In an emergency bear left at the ruins, heading straight downhill, which will take you back to the main road.

11. **Pass the ruins on your right. The path then starts to lead slightly
uphill, passing between two hillocks and leading to a stony
trackway. Bear left and follow the track as it winds downhill.**

☺ There is no more climbing now. The rest of the walk is either downhill or
flat. Soon the sea and the beach should come into view straight ahead,
and that's where you're heading. See if you can spot any ships out at
sea.

12. **Go through the metal gate at the bottom and carefully cross the
road. To the left of the small car park opposite is a signed footpath. Go through the metal gate and follow the track leading
downhill.**

☺ There are many bushes and plants on both sides of the path now. One
bush has long clusters of purple flowers in the summer. It is called a
"buddleia" and attracts many butterflies, so it is often called a "butterfly
bush".

Ahead the footpath crosses a railway line. This is a proper crossing
place, so cross carefully, as the sign says: "stop, look, listen, beware of
trains" and never play on railways.

13. **Keeping children under close control go through the kissing gate
and carefully cross over the railway at the crossing point. Go
through the kissing gate opposite and continue ahead.**

☺ This is now a golf course. You may see coloured flags flying, which
show the golfers where the next hole is. You are getting closer to the
sea all the time, and should by now be able to hear the sound of waves.

14. **The path winds through an area of reeds and flowers and crosses
over a drainage ditch. Continue straight ahead through the
sandhills.**

☺ In the sandhills turn round and look back. You should be able to see the cemetery and the path you walked along over the hills.

15. **Turn left and make your way along the beach. (This is the only direction you'll need for over a mile.)**

☺ The rest of the walk is along this wide sandy beach, so you can take your time and do all the things you like to do at the seaside: make sandcastles, collect shells, paddle or just sunbathe.

As the beach curves around to the left Aberdyfi should come into view again.

To return to the railway station look out for the flagpole and life belt holder in the sandhills (after 1 mile along the beach). Here bear left through the sandhills and follow the clear path. Keep straight ahead and pass under the arched railway bridge. Bear immediately left after the bridge and keep straight ahead.

16. **To return to Aberdyfi keep ahead along the beach, until the town and amenities come into view.**

Aberdyfi Checklist

☐ A BOAT

☐ A SEAGULL

☐ A SHEEP

☐ A TRACTOR

☐ A COW

☐ A SHELL

☐ A BEACHBALL

☐ A PLANT WITH PRICKLES

☐ A BUCKET AND SPADE

☐ A CARAVAN

☐ A DOG

☐ SOMEBODY WATERSKIING

Dyfi Valley: Pennal

This is a moderate walk: fairly long, but relatively flat, much of it along the lonely banks of the afon Dyfi, where you might not see a soul for hours. The Dyfi valley is a beautiful area, but this particular part, sadly, has many of its footpaths blocked or missing altogether, with very few signs and often stiles missing or damaged. The footpaths marked on your map won't help you very much, because in reality many of them just aren't there anymore, and I spent several hours trying to find my way back to the campsite where I was staying. This route, however, (at the time of writing) gave no problems, except that there was a lack of signposts.

Starting Point: Outside the pub in the centre of Pennal village (SH699004) on the A487, 7 miles east of Aberdyfi.

By Bus: Services from Machynlleth and Tywyn.

Car Parking: There is no car park in the village, except the pub car park, which is for patrons only. If you do find somewhere to wedge your car in, please make sure you have parked considerately. There are parking lay-bys on the main road just before and after the village.

Distance: 5 miles.

Terrain: No severe climbs. Footpaths mainly, a few stretches along quiet lanes.

Maps: As mentioned in the introduction, many of the public footpaths in this area are illegally blocked, so half those shown criss-crossing this area just don't exist. However, it's always handy to carry a map. OS Landranger 135 or OS Outdoor Leisure 23.

Public Toilets: Pennal village, along the lane opposite the pub, on the left.

Refreshments: Pub in Pennal, which also does "orning Coffee". (The "M" had fallen off.) Talgarth Hall, pub, restaurant, open to non-residents.

☺ This little village is called Pennal. It has a pub, a church (Saint Peter in chains) and a Post Office. Look for one of the houses which is covered in model butterflies.

Q: What is the name of the pub in the village?
A: The Riverside Hotel.

Pennal village

1. **Standing outside the pub, facing the church, bear left, passing the pub car park and carefully cross the bridge.**

Q: There are two dates on the old stone bridge. What are they?

A: 1610 and 1987.

2. **Continue along the lane, passing the Post Office and school. Go through the gate on the left, signed as a public footpath and follow the stony trackway.**

☺ On your left is the afon (River) Pennal which brings the water down from the surrounding hills. To the left you should be able to see the high mountains of central Snowdonia. The peaks might have snow on them, or might be hidden in the cloud.

3. **Go through the gateway barring the track and continue ahead.**

☺ Notice the "ford" across the river. This is a shallow part where a track or lane crosses over.

4. **Go through the next gate and follow the track to the left. Keep to the main track leading straight ahead, and avoid gates and tracks to either side.**

Q: There are brambles, hawthorn and gorse bushes growing along the track now. All of these bushes have prickles or thorns, but one of them has yellow flowers in the summer. Do you know which one?

A: Gorse. Brambles and hawthorn have white or pink flowers in the spring.

5.   Go through further gates until you get to the afon Dyfi. Bear right along the clear trackway.

☺ This is the afon (River) Dyfi, which the whole valley is named after. It is the biggest river in the area, and all the other smaller rivers join it. The afon Dyfi joins the sea at the seaside town of Aberdyfi, which means "mouth of the river Dyfi".

The river is deep and wide here, so don't go near the edges.

6.   Keep along the raised bank with the path on top. It doesn't run directly alongside the water's edge all the way, but is very easy to follow.

☺ To your right you should be able to see over reeds and marshes to flat fields which might have cows or sheep in them. At one time these fields were very boggy and covered with prickly bushes and weeds, but now this bank keeps back a lot of the floodwater, and the fields have been cleared.

7.   Cross the various stiles and keep straight ahead along the raised bank.

☺ When the river gets very high pieces of driftwood and bottles get washed-up onto the bank. Can you see any bottles left here by the river?

You may see ducks, geese or swans on the water. These are all waterbirds. You might also see seagulls, who often fly inland when the weather is bad.

On your left, on the other side of the river is a railway line. Look for the viaduct ahead, where the line crosses the river.

Alternative route: The same distance, but more sheltered. On the right is a track leading down to a gate and stile. Here there is a notice about the permitted path to Yr Ynys. Cross the stile. Once over, the path bears around to the right, away from the river. Keep straight ahead, go through the gate then bear left along the gravelled track. Bear right at the farm and rejoin the route at Direction 10.

8. Continue along the riverbank.

☺ You should by now have a good view of the viaduct on the left, and might be lucky enough to see a train crossing.

Q: Look for the stone cottage in the trees on the right. How many chimneys does it have?

A: Three.

9. Look out for the wooden footbridge to the right. Go down the bank, cross over the drainage ditch and keep ahead along the side of the field, now with a drainage ditch on your left. When you come to the crossing place cross over, go through the gate and bear diagonally right towards the farm buildings. Join the rough trackway and continue towards the farm.

10. Follow the farm driveway, passing the farmhouse on your left and continue along the lane leading uphill.

☺ As you get higher up the lane there are views to the right over the river and the path you have walked along. You can see the flat fields on either side of the water, and several wide bends in the river, which are called "meanders".

11. Avoid trackways and drives to either side. Keep with the lane.

☺ You are now walking through very nice countryside, of fields and woodlands. There may be horses in some of the fields. You should pass a "bungalow" along the lane. This is a house all on one floor, so there is no upstairs.

Escape route: To cut off a slight corner, on the right after the bungalow is a gate with a stile next to it, currently unsigned. Cross over and bear straight ahead, uphill, towards the hotel buildings. Continue from Direction 13.)

12. Continue ahead along the lane until you come to a driveway leading off to the right, signed as Penmaendyfi. Follow the driveway uphill until you come to the hotel and other buildings.

At the time of writing there are no signs to help you through the hotel grounds, but this will hopefully soon be corrected when new management take over. A clear driveway leads between the main hotel buildings, which is the most direct route, though this is not the official footpath. I was told by the then owner it was perfectly acceptable to wander around the hotel grounds at will, but the following directions are based on the current OS map having the correct Right of Way.

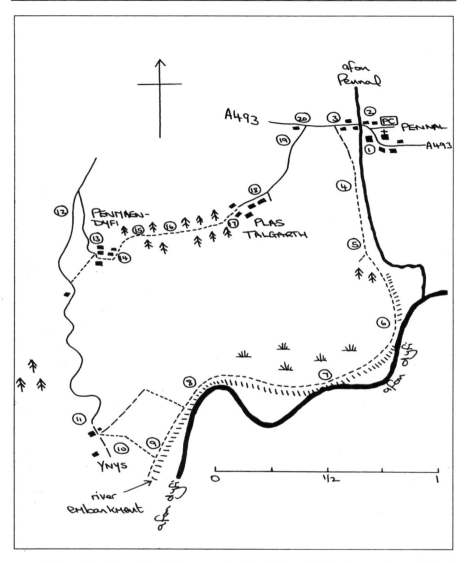

13.   **There is a large building on the far right. To the immediate left of
      this is an unsigned pathway. Follow this between the swimming
      pool and terrace. At the end bear left over the grass, leading up-
      hill. Keep ahead until you arrive at the gravel driveway. To the
      right there is a gate into a field.**

14. **Go through the gate and turn left, uphill. Head for the trees in the top right hand corner of the field.**

☺ From here there are good views over the river and railway viaduct that you passed earlier. Further up the hill you should be able to see where the river joins the sea near Aberdyfi.

15. **At the top go through the metal gate, signed with an arrow, and follow the clear path ahead, slightly downhill through beech woodland.**

☺ Look out for squirrels amongst the trees. Notice that some of the trees have nesting boxes on them, where birds can build nests and lay eggs. You might be lucky enough to see an owl, especially in the evening. (I did!)

16. **At the end of the woods climb the stile and keep straight ahead across the grassy field. Cross a further stile into the woods again. Avoid the steps off to the right, and keep straight ahead. Take care to avoid all minor turnings off the main pathway.**

17. **At the bottom bear left onto the wide trackway, heading towards the buildings. Keep straight ahead along the driveway leading downhill through the holiday village grounds, passing a pitch and putt course on the left. At the junction head straight across. Follow the main driveway.**

This is all part of Talgarth Hotel, where the facilities are open to non-residents. The main building, a Georgian mansion, can be found to the right.

18. **Keep left at the next junction, following the main driveway.**

Q: You may see a round road sign with the number 15 on it. What do you think this means?

A: It is telling drivers that they must not drive faster than 15 miles an hour. (It's unlikely you'll be able to reach that speed on your feet!)

19. **Go through the gates and bear right along the edge of the road.**

Q: What stone animals can you spot at the gates?

A: There is a lion on the top of each gatepost.

20. **This is now the outskirts of Pennal village. Continue ahead across the bridge to the village centre to finish the route.**

Pennal Checklist

- [ ] A WHITE COTTAGE
- [ ] A CHURCH
- [ ] A HORSE
- [ ] A STONE BRIDGE
- [ ] A WOODEN BRIDGE
- [ ] A BLACK COW
- [ ] A BROWN COW
- [ ] A WHITE SHEEP
- [ ] A BLACK SHEEP
- [ ] A SEAGULL
- [ ] A HERON
- [ ] A TRACTOR
- [ ] A TRAIN
- [ ] A HEN

Walks around
Harlech to Llanbedr

Harlech is best known for its castle, built by Edward I, and its song, "Men of Harlech". It is a small place with a few shops and a few cafés (see Harlech route). There is a wide sandy beach below, quite a trek across a golf course and through sandhills.

Further south along the main road is Llanfair, a small scattered village. On the right is a turning down to the station and beach,

Harlech: the castle and rooftops

where there is a small shop and café. To the left look out for "Chwarel Hen Llanfair" (Llanfair Old Quarry) where there are tours down into a slate mine, also has a souvenir shop and café (see Llandanwg route).

Continuing south you will come to the village of Llanbedr alongside the afon Artro. There is a pub on the main road, and a couple of restaurants about the village. There are walks along the attractive river valley and through the forest (see the River Artro route). Also close by is Maes Artro, (on the right after the village) which is a collection of workshops, museums and amenities. Shell Island (bear right after the river) where there are further tourist amenities and hundreds of shells for the taking.

Faithful companion on the beach at Llandanwg

Harlech To Llanbedr: Harlech

A short, moderately easy route based around Harlech and its immediate countryside. Good views of the castle and out to sea. The castle and a small playground are passed on the route.

Starting Point: The front of the castle, Harlech (SH582313) off the B4573

By Bus: Regular services from Blaenau Ffestiniog (mainline rail connection from the north-west) and Barmouth.

By Rail: From Harlech Station head uphill to the castle.

Car Parking: There is a small car park at the Starting Point, in front of the castle, signed from the High Street (B4573). There are also various other car parks in Harlech, all well signed.

Distance: 1½ miles.

Terrain: Mainly good footpaths, with some steady uphill stretches. Also a short distance along a quiet lane.

Maps: OS Landranger 24, OS Outdoor Leisure 18.

Public Toilets: Turn right out of the castle car park. The toilets are on the left, opposite the statue.

Refreshments: In the town centre.

☺ Harlech Castle was built over 700 years ago, so it is very old. At the time it stood at the edge of the sea, but now the sea is further away, and there are sand dunes between the castle and the sea.

1. **Facing the castle bear right, towards the castle entrance, where there is a small children's playground. Go along the pathway alongside the playground. At the end bear left onto the lane, leading downhill between cottages.**

2. **Take the signed footpath off to the right, along a trackway which leads uphill.**

☺ There are plants along the sides of the paths such as brambles and nettles. As the path climbs higher there are views to the distance, and you might be able to see the sea.

3. Take care of children, as the steps at the end of the path lead up to a road. Carefully cross over the road and take the footpath directly opposite, leading up further steps. Continue along the pathway (which splits and rejoins at the grassy area, so either turning will do). At the top of the path bear left along the wide trackway.

Escape route: Bear right onto the track, passing the chapel, then right again, follow the lane downhill and cross the road to the castle and Starting Point.)

4. Follow the stony trackway which starts to lead downhill.

Q: You should soon pass a stone house on the left. How many chimneys does it have?

A: Three

5. Look out for the signed footpath off to the left and follow it downhill.

☺ The path leads between many bushes and trees, including rhododendrons, which are the bushes with large, oval leaves, which have large clusters of colourful flowers in the summer. Look out on the left for the unusual round house with a chimney in the middle of the roof.

There are now woods on the left. Many of the trees are oaks. Keep a look out on the ground for acorns, which are the fruit of the oak tree. Between the trees on the left you should sometimes be able to see the sea.

There are stone walls along the path in places, which have ivy, moss and small ferns growing on them. The gaps between the stones make cool, shady places for insects to hide.

Q: There are many insects living in the woods, such as beetles, butterflies and bees. Which of these insects makes honey?

A: Bees make honey for their young to eat.

6. The path leads onto a tarmac drive. From the drive bear right, signed as a footpath, passing a set of stone steps leading up to a white stone house. Go through the metal gate and follow the grassy path.

Q: There are still woodlands down on the left. As well as being the home of many insects, the woods are very popular with birds. Sparrows, crows, magpies, and pigeons are often found in woods. Which of these birds are all black?

A: Crows are all black.

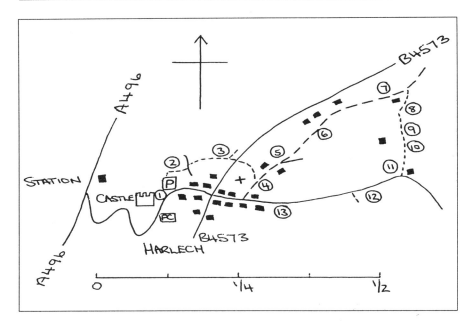

7. **Go through the next gateway and continue ahead, then bear right at the signed footpath, leading uphill, now passing behind the white house.**

☺ As you get higher there are views of the castle on your right and out to sea. Can you see any ships?

8. **Go through the open gateway straight ahead. Keep with the wall.**

☺ Take a moment to look back at the view. Can you see the island in the "estuary" of the river? An estuary is the wide part of a river, just before it joins the sea.

9. **Go through another open gateway. Again keep with the wall.**

☺ There might be sheep in this field, or cows. If you look behind you there is the ruin of an old farmhouse.

10. **Avoid the gateway to the right. Keep straight ahead with the wall.**

☺ The chimneys of a house should come into view ahead. You should be walking towards them.

11. **Go through the gate into the farmyard and follow the driveway which bears around to the right, so you pass the farmhouse on your left. Bear right along the narrow lane. (The road is very quiet, but beware of any vehicles.)**

Q: On the right, at the top of the hill there is a farmhouse with two chimneys. How many windows are there upstairs in the farmhouse?

A: From here there are three.

☺ On your left you should pass what looks like a square stone "pond" which was built in 1841. Can you work out how long ago that was?

12. **Avoid the footpath to the right. Continue along the lane.**

☺ It is now downhill all the way back. You should soon be able to see the town of Harlech straight ahead of you.

Q: At the end of this road you should pass a pub named after an animal. What is it called?

A: The Lion Hotel.

13. **Cross the road and continue ahead to the castle and Starting Point.**

Harlech Checklist

☐ A FLAG

☐ A STATUE

☐ A SHEEP

☐ A COW

☐ A SEAGULL

☐ A PINK FLOWER IN SPRING

☐ AN ACORN

☐ A BOAT

☐ A CARAVAN

☐ A STINGING NETTLE

☐ A WHITE HOUSE

☐ A BLACK BIRD

Harlech to Llanbedr: Llandanwg

Quite a popular little place where there is a good beach, estuary marshes for the birdwatcher, attractive countryside and even an optional visit to a slate cavern. (Chwarel Hen Llanfair, open daily from Easter to October.)

Starting Point: The car park, Llandanwg (SH568283). One mile south of Harlech, in Llanfair, there is a small road leading towards the sea, well-signed as leading to a car park. Follow this right to the end.

By Rail: Trains running along the coast between Pwllheli and Aberystwyth via Harlech, stop at Llandanwg. There is a stile on each side of the railway. Make sure the road bridge is on your left, climb the stile and continue from Direction 4.

Distance: Just over 2½ miles, but with no Escape Route, except to return by train.

Terrain: Moderate. Public footpaths and quiet lanes. Some uphill stretches, but nothing too steep. The footpaths, however, do cross a railway line twice, which presents no threat if care is taken.

Maps: OS Landranger 124, OS Outdoor Leisure 18.

Public Toilets: In the car park.

Refreshments: Small beach café and shop in the car park. Café at the slate caverns, about half way round the route.

---

1. **From the car park return along the road. There is a pavement on the left.**

☺ There are houses along this road, some of them don't have an upstairs, so the bedrooms are downstairs as well. A house with no upstairs is called a "bungalow".

Q: Look out for the post box in the wall on the left. What are the gold letters in the middle of it?

A: E II R, which means Elizabeth II Regina, which is Latin for Queen Elizabeth II, the present queen.

2. **Look out for the signed footpath off to the right. Climb the steps over the wall, go through the gate and descend the steps into the field. Keep left along the edge of the field.**

☺ There might be cows or sheep in any of the walled fields at this part of the walk. Most of the sheep will be white, but there can be brown or black ones. See if you can spot any.

3. **Climb the stile and taking great care cross the railway line. Climb the stile opposite and continue ahead.**

☺ You have probably been taught not to play on or near railways, because they can be very dangerous. Here the footpath crosses the railway, so you should take great care, and as the sign says "Stop, look and listen" before you cross, and never cross without a grown-up to help you.

4. **Go up the steps, through the gap in the stone wall and bear left, following the wall.**

5. **Avoid the steps and the gate in the corner. Continue around the corner of the field to a further set of steps leading to a gate over the wall. Bear right on the other side with the wall on your right. At the corner bear left, now walking along a grassy lane between drystone walls, starting to lead gradually uphill.**

☺ As the path leads you higher you should be able to look back and see sandhills and then the sea, and the sound of waves should be getting quieter as you get further away from the beach. Perhaps you will see a train going along the railway line.

6. **Look out for the steps in the wall on the right, cross over and head across the field towards the farmhouse.**

Q: Look at the farmhouse across the field. How many chimneys are there on the main roof?

A: Four

7. **On the other side of the field bear left along the gravel trackway, passing the farmhouse on your right. After the farm bear right through one of the gateways and cross the grassy field. Stride over the small stream and head for the metal gate in the far left corner.**

8. **Go through the gate and bear right onto the quiet lane. After about 20 yards bear left through a small metal gate. Keep left along the edge of the field.**

☺ There are views to the right over the estuary of the River Artro. An "estuary" is the last part of a river's journey, just before it reaches the sea, and

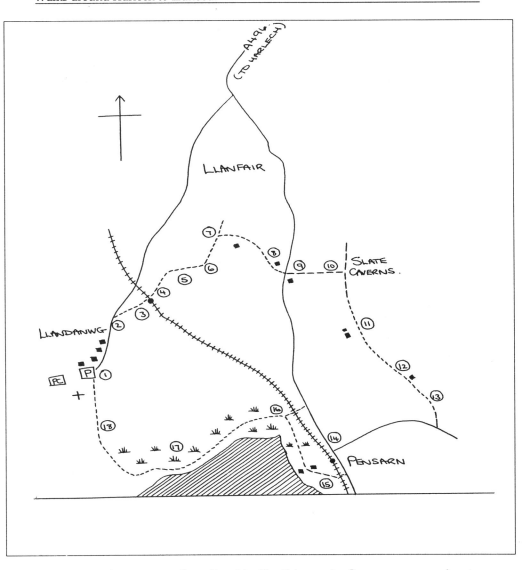

estuaries are usually quite wide, like this one is. Can you see any boats on the water?

There are houses to your left. One of them has a "Weathervane" on the roof. Can you spot it? A weathervane shows which direction the wind is blowing.

9. **Go through the gateway into a further field and keep left until you come to another gate which will lead you onto the road. Bear left along the pavement and carefully cross over to the driveway of "Chwarel Hen Llanfair" (slate cavern), which is a well-used but unsigned public path. Pass the stables and farmhouse on the right. Go through the gateway and continue straight ahead.**

☺ On the hillside ahead you should be able to see heaps of loose grey stone. This is slate, which has been dug out of the ground. It is a very common stone in this part of Wales and is often used for building. Look around and see if you can spot any buildings made of it.

10. **Bear right at the junction and follow the stony trackway. (Take care as in places there is a slight drop to the right of the path, so keep younger children under control.)**

    (The cavern, café and shop are all off to the left at the junction.)

Q: There may well be ducks, hens, peacocks and other birds along this path, some of them loose, so keep dogs on a lead, and others in pens. Which of these birds is famous for its long, colourful tail feathers?

A: The peacock.

11. **Go through the gateway and continue ahead along the path, which is now narrower and starts to lead downhill. Go through a further gate and again keep straight ahead, passing various farm buildings on your right.**

☺ It is often muddy here, so look out for footprints on the ground. They might be made by sheep, cows, horses, dogs or people. See if you can tell which is which.

12. **If you keep ahead a grassy path starts to lead uphill and a wall begins on the right. Keep straight ahead and a house should come into view. Go through the gate right in front of the house, passing the front door, and go through a further gate opposite and follow the driveway leading steeply downhill.**

☺ This lane goes downhill quite steeply, so go carefully. Sometimes it can be nearly as difficult going downhill as uphill. The wall and some of the trees might have ivy growing on them. Ivy is a climbing plant and has tiny suckers which it can attach to things to help it climb.

13. **At the bottom bear right, crossing a cattle grid, and follow the narrow lane leading further downhill. Bear right at the junction.**

(This is a fairly quiet lane, but do be aware of any approaching vehicles.)

☺ When you are walking along a road keep as close to the edge as you can. Cars in Britain drive on the left, so you should always walk FACING the traffic, so you can see what is approaching and will know if you need to step out of the way.

Q: On the right look out for a name plate at the gate of one of the houses, which says Pensarn Hall. What is the date underneath, which is when the house was built?

A: 1895.

14. **Bear left at the bottom of the lane. Cross over when appropriate and bear right, signed for the station. Carefully cross over the railway line and go through the gate opposite. (To cut the route short catch the train for one stop, back to Llandanwg and retrace your steps for the Starting Point.)**

☺ Remember, as the sign says, to "Stop, look and listen" before you cross the railway track. This will bring you to Pensarn Harbour, where there will probably be many boats.

15. **From the gate follow the driveway leading right in front of the buildings, go under the two arches and through the gateway at the end, onto a flat grassy area alongside the estuary. Bear diagonally right, towards the gate by the railway line.**

☺ This part of the river estuary is "tidal", which means that the sea reaches this far when it comes in. When the tide is very high this area can be flooded and all sorts of litter from the sea gets washed up here. See if you can spot: the branch of a tree, a ball, a plastic bottle, a seashell, a drinks can and a shoe.

16. **Do not go through the gate to the railway. Instead continue along the railway embankment, with the tracks on your right. Cross the bridge over the stream which comes from beneath the embankment. Climb the steps and bear left along the grassy bank, which now leads away from the railway.**

☺ This bank was built to try and keep the sea and the river from flooding the land on your right, but in very bad conditions the grassy fields still get waterlogged. In the distance towards the right see if you can spot a small church which is near the car park, where the walk started.

Looking back at this point you should be able to see the slate mine and the countryside which you have walked through. Ahead the sound of the sea should be getting louder, and you may see or hear the calling of seagulls.

17. Go through the metal kissing gate, cross over the drainage channel and follow the path around to the right. Keep with the drainage channel.

☺ Over on the left you should see the little church, which often gets half buried in the sand dunes, when the wind blows the sand about. Can you see the bell on the roof of the church?

18. The drainage channel will bring you to a kissing gate, keep left which will take you back to the car park.

Llandanwg Checklist

☐ A WOODEN GATE

☐ A SHEEP

☐ A WHITE HOUSE

☐ A PEACOCK

☐ A BOAT WITH A SAIL

☐ A TRAIN

☐ A SEAGULL

☐ A METAL GATE

☐ A COW

☐ A DUCK

☐ A WATERFALL

☐ A BOAT WITHOUT A SAIL

☐ A CHURCH

Harlech To Llanbedr:
Llanbedr & The River Artro

A really enjoyable walk, and apart from three short uphill stretches it is fairly easy going. Don't let the length put you off. There are various Escape Routes and the walk can be split in half to make a good 2½ mile circular route. The banks of the River Artro here are thickly wooded and a haven for wildlife.

Close to Llanbedr is the Maes Artro village, where there are museums, displays, crafts and a walk-through badger hole. Also Shell Island, where up to 200 types of weird and wonderful shells get washed-up onto the beach, plus a tavern, restaurant and snack bar. Open from March to October. Signed from the village.

Starting Point: The bridge over the River Artro, on the A496, Llanbedr (SH585268)

By Bus: Buses from Barmouth, Harlech and Blaenau stop outside the pub right next to the Starting Point.

By Rail: Head inland, along the lane, passing the car park and the lane soon joins the river and heads directly into the village. A walk of less than half a mile.

Car Parking: If approaching along the main road from Harlech, bear right in Llanbedr directly after crossing the river, signed for Shell Island. After a third of a mile there is a car park on the right. Walk back to the bridge to start the walk.

Distance: 5 miles, several Escape Routes.

Terrain: Quiet forest roadways and public footpaths. Some uphill sections but nothing too difficult.

Public Toilets: Towards the end of the route. From the Starting Point cross over the bridge and bear right after the pub. The toilets are on the right.

Refreshments: Village pub, Aber Artro Hall Tea-room.

---

1. **From the side of the bridge that has a seating area go down the steps next to the river, signed as a footpath, and follow the riverside path.**

☺ This is the River (or "afon") Artro, which brings water down from the surrounding hills and mountains and takes it to the sea not far from here.

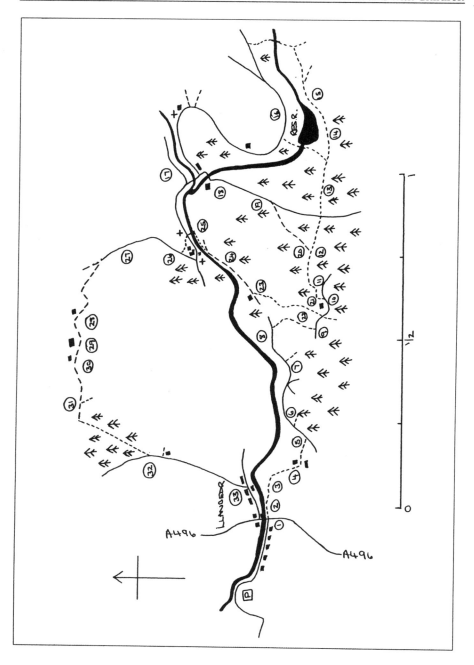

You are now walking "upstream", which means you are heading against the flow of the water.

2. **Go through the kissing gate and keep left along the edge of the field, passing the small playground. Avoid the paths leading up-hill towards the houses.**

3. **Pass the playing fields on the right, then go through a further kissing gate. Bear right along the edge of the field.**

Q: There may be cows in this field. Cows are female. Do you know what the males are called?

A: Bulls.

4. **Go through the metal gate signed with an arrow, passing the large house on your left. Continue ahead towards the stables. Bear left and go through the long metal gate. Follow the stony trackway between the farm buildings, which starts to lead uphill.**

☺ At the farm look out for the hay-barn, where hay can be stored and kept dry. In the winter it is used for bedding and food for animals.

There are many rabbits in the area, so keep a look out for a flash of their white tails as they run for cover as you approach.

5. **Bear left onto the road.**

☺ This quiet roadway is shaded with overhanging trees. The river should now be close on your left. Keep a look out for squirrels amongst the trees.

6. **Avoid the footpath to the right. At the fork, keep left with the river.**

☺ You will soon cross over a bridge. Underneath it a waterfall gushes down into the river.

7. **Continue ahead, avoiding the footpath to the right.**

☺ There are many silver birch trees in the woods now. They are easy to recognise with their slim, white trunks. See if you can spot any. The path soon crosses another bridge over a smaller stream.

8. **After the second bridge the roadway bears to the right and then the left, at which point bear right along the signed footpath leading into the woods.**

☺ In the woods look out for rowan trees, which have orange-red berries in the late summer. Also look out for prickly holly, which has dark red berries in the autumn. Birds and small animals can eat berries like these, which are brightly coloured, so they can easily be spotted, even after snow. Because animals eat berries and wild fruit, it doesn't mean they are safe for people to eat. Never touch wild berries, as many can be poisonous to people.

9. **At the top of the woods bear left along the lane. Avoid the footpaths to both sides. Continue ahead.**

Escape route: To cut the route in half, bear left along the signed footpath leading back down into the woods, and skip to Direction 22.

Q: A large stone house should come into view ahead, which you will pass on the left. What is it called? Look for the sign.
A: Craig Artro.

10. **Directly after the house bear left along the footpath. Go through the gate and onto Woodland Trust land. Follow the main stony trackway. Where the track splits keep left, along the lower track.**

☺ There are many birds living in these woods. You can probably hear them singing in the treetops. See if you can spot any nests among the branches.

11. **Avoid the minor grassy track to the left. Continue ahead.**

Q: There are many different trees in the woods, including sycamore, oak and beech. Can you recognise them? In the autumn these trees all produce very different types of seeds. Do you know what the seed of the oak tree is called?
A: An acorn.

12. **Keep straight ahead, avoiding a further path to the left. The track starts to lead uphill. When you come to the lane go straight across onto further Woodland Trust land.**

(There should be a notice board to the left giving information about the site, and warning that there is a steep sided gorge ahead which may be hazardous "especially to children". As long as you stick to the main path you won't come anywhere near the gorge, but do keep small children and dogs under control anyway.)

Escape route: As the small reservoir comes into view ahead bear left along the path and follow it down to the dam. Cross over the footbridge and carry on up the steps. Keep ahead until you come to the lane, then bear left. Continue after Direction 15.

13. Keep straight ahead through the woods and go through the gate barring the trackway.

☺ Below on the left, through the trees, you should be able to see a small reservoir". A reservoir is a lake made by blocking a stream or river, where water can be stored until it is needed. The water that comes out of your taps at home comes from large reservoirs that often fill whole valleys.

14. Go through a further gate and continue ahead.

Q: There are now views of high hills. Look straight ahead into the distance. Can you see the white cottage? How many chimneys does it have?

A: Two

15. The trees end and the path leads through an area of bracken. When the path splits bear left, signed with occasional arrows. Cross the footbridge and continue straight ahead through the tall oak trees to the lane. Bear left. At the junction keep left. (This is a quiet lane but beware of any approaching traffic. There is plenty of room on both sides to walk on the grass if you prefer. In places there are steep drops in the woods, down to the river, so again keep children and dogs under close control.)

Q: You should be able to see the small reservoir again below, and later hear the rushing of the stream. Before long you should pass a house on the right, which has several tall chimneys, and soon after look out for a triangular road sign with a horse and rider on it. What do you think this means?

A: Most triangular signs are warnings. This one is warning motorists that there may be horse riders along the lane.

☺ On the right there are fields with stone walls, where there might be sheep grazing. There is a farmhouse in the distance. See if you can spot a tractor in any of the fields.

16. Avoid the driveway leading off to the left. The road leads down-hill. Avoid two footpaths off to the right. Keep left with the lane.

☺ The building on the right is a chapel, which is like a small church. There is a graveyard in front of it, with slate headstones.

The lane leads downhill and a different river runs close by on the right.

Look out for the small tree-covered island. This smaller river joins the River Artro just ahead, close to the bridge.

There is a row of stone cottages on the left. The last one has a white "dovecote" on its side wall, which is where doves can shelter. Doves are related to pigeons and are often, but not always, completely white.

17. Cross over the cattle grid and continue to the junction. Bear left.

Q: Look at the various road signs at the junction. How far is Llanbedr from here?

A: 1 mile

Escape route: In an emergency bear right instead, which will take you back to Llanbedr, but bear in mind that it is a busier road.

Q: You are now back with the River Artro. Look over the wall on the right and see if you can see the arched stone bridge crossing the river. What date is shown on the bridge?

A: 1837

18. Cross the bridge, after which the lane starts to lead quite steeply uphill.

Q: Once you have crossed the bridge look at the stone building on the right. What is it called?

A: There is a sign on the front of the building and at the gate. It is called Aber Artro Hall.

(The gardens and tea-room are open Sundays to Wednesdays, from 11 am to 5 p.m. No dogs allowed.)

☺ After the hall the road starts to lead uphill quite steeply. Just take your time and it won't seem so bad. The sound of water gets fainter as you get further away from the river below. Notice that there are grassy banks at the sides of the road with roots showing through from the many trees that grow here. Roots bring water and food to feed the tree. The roots can spread for quite a distance underground.

19. At the top of the steepest part you should come to another Woodland Trust sign on the right. Here follow the clear level trackway leading through the trees. Keep left at the junction.

☺ There are several holly bushes in this part of the woods. As you will know, holly has dark, prickly leaves, which are used at Christmas in decorations.

If it is autumn, see how many different sorts of leaves you can find on the ground.

20. **When you come to it, pick your way over the small stream which crosses the path. Then at the T-junction, bear right.**

☺ You may recognise this path from earlier in the walk. You are now walking the opposite way through the woods. Keep a look out for squirrels, and see how many birds you can spot.

21. **Keep to the main trackway. Avoid the path to the left. Return the same way, going through the gate and dropping down to the lane. Bear right, passing the house on the right. Bear right along the first signed footpath.**

Escape route: Continue ahead along the lane, and when you arrive down at the river keep right, bearing right along the farm trackway and following the footpath back to the Starting Point.

22. **Follow the pathway downhill through the woods.**

☺ This stony path leads downhill through the woods. Take care as you cross the wet area. If you look up to the right you might be able to see the chimneys of Craig Artro.

23. **The footpath is easy to follow. Cross the slate slab bridge and go through the gap in the wall, heading towards farm buildings. Bear right along the farm driveway, which becomes a stony track running alongside the river. Go through the gate into the woods. (The lower gate, not the gate into the field.)**

☺ You should now be walking alongside the river again. At this point there is a tree-covered island in the middle of the water. Can you see it?

24. **Keep left, following the riverside footpath and cross the footbridge.**

☺ While crossing the bridge stop and look over at the river. The water is clear and you can see the stones on the bottom. Can you see any fish?

25. **Go up the steps and carefully bear right along the road. Between the phone box and the chapel there is a small gate. Go through and follow the narrow pathway leading slightly uphill, with a wall on your right and fenced bushes on your left. At the top the footpath passes through the grounds of a house. Bear right be-**

tween the buildings, go through the gates and bear right along the
lane.

(This footpath is currently unsigned. If you don't spot it, you can
bear left along the lane from the bridge, taking care at the bends,
keep well in. When you come to another chapel on the left, bear
right and keep straight ahead. You are now back with the route.)

26. **Follow the lane as it leads uphill.**

☺ There are good views to the right over the wall, of fields where there
may be sheep, to the high hills in the distance.

27. **Cross the cattle grid and continue ahead. The road now becomes
a stony trackway. Where the track splits bear left.**

☺ This is now the highest part of the walk, so it is level or downhill for the
rest of the way. You should pass a small house on the right, then go
through a set of stone gateposts. Farm buildings should come into view
ahead.

28. **Cross the cattle grid and pass the back of the farm house.**

☺ Notice the farmhouse is built of stone, but three of the four chimneys are
made of brick and were probably added later.

Q: On the left there are some old, overgrown tennis courts. Do you know
what the "bat" used in tennis is called?
A: A "racquet".

29. **When the tarmac drive bears around to the right to another house
keep straight ahead along the stony trackway. There should be a
stone wall on your left.**

☺ In wet weather it might be muddy here. See if you can find any footprints
on the ground, not only left by other people, but also animals, such as
cows, sheep and horses.

30. **Go through the kissing gate and continue ahead. There is still a
wall on the left. Keep with this wall at all times and avoid the
track that bears off to the right.**

☺ You should soon have views of the "estuary" of the River Artro. This is
the point where a river joins the sea. Can you see any ships out at sea?
Look out for the railway viaduct crossing the river, with its many arches.

31. **The path starts to drop downhill. Keep with the wall and avoid the footpath over the wall to the left. Follow the wall around to the left and go through the gate into the woods.**

☺ Many of the trees in the woods have ivy growing on them. Ivy is a climbing plant which has tiny suckers so it can cling to the tree trunks or walls.

32. **At the bottom of the path bear left along the lane. At the T-junction bear right and follow the pavement.**

☺ You are now coming towards the end of the walk, passing hotels and restaurants on the edge of the village. Over on the left is the River Artro again.

(The public toilets are on the left of this road. At the corner the pub has a large beer garden and children's play area.)

33. **Bear left in the village and return to the bridge over the river, which was the Starting Point.**

Woodland trackway near the River Artro

River Artro Checklist

- ☐ A PLANE
- ☐ A STONE BRIDGE
- ☐ AN ACORN
- ☐ A SYCAMORE KEY
- ☐ A BEECHNUT
- ☐ A BLACK BIRD
- ☐ A DOG
- ☐ A SHEEP
- ☐ A SQUIRREL
- ☐ A BUSH WITH PRICKLES
- ☐ A COW
- ☐ A TRACTOR
- ☐ THE SEA

Walks around Llanberis

Llanberis is situated at the foot of Snowdon itself, and is a popular base for walkers and climbers. It is also the start of the famous Snowdon Mountain Railway, which will take you to the very top of the mountain: all the views, none of the effort.

Llanberis was once a slate quarrying community. The quarry scars are still clearly visible, but the town now aims itself at the visitor. It lies on the shores of Llyn Padarn, where there are boats for hire. It has restaurants, pubs, cafés, gift shops, a castle, a hydro-electric power station concealed underground (interesting tours available from "Electric Mountain" next to the main car park in the centre of the village) and a pleasant Country Park adapted from the old quarrying site (see Llyn Padarn route). Here you will find the Llanberis Lake Railway, steaming up and down one side of Llyn Padarn. The area was popular with the Victorians for its views and waterfalls (see Dolbadarn route).

The road leading up to the Llanberis Pass

Llanberis:
Dolbadarn Castle & The Waterfalls

*A short and easy walk taking in many of the attractions of Llanberis,
including the castle, the waterfalls, Snowdon Mountain Railway, the
lake and Padarn Country Park.*

Starting Point: Dolbadarn Castle car park (SH584599). Signed for the castle, off
the main road.

By Bus: Services from Caernarfon, Bangor, Betws-y-Coed and Beddgelert.

Car Parking: At the Starting Point, or any of the other car parks in the village, or
at Padarn Country Park. All well-signed.

Distance: 2 miles.

Terrain: Footpaths and pavements. Some uphill stretches, but nothing severe.

Maps: OS Landranger 115, OS Outdoor Leisure 17.

Public Toilets: Various places in the village.

Refreshments: Various places.

---

1. **Leave the main entrance to Dolbadarn car park and carefully
    cross the road. Bear left along the pavement. After a few yards
    bear right, crossing the footbridge over the river. Go through the
    kissing gate and follow the pathway leading slightly uphill. Keep
    to the left and the castle should come into view ahead.**

☺   The trees in these woods are mainly oaks. Look out for acorns on the
    ground. Acorns are the seeds of the oak tree, and can grow into an oak
    "sapling". A sapling is a young tree.

    Ahead is Dolbadarn Castle, which was built over 800 years ago. It was
    built here on this rocky outcrop, so there was a good view in both direc-
    tions along the valley.

*To visit the castle go through the gap in the drystone wall and continue
ahead. But return the same way, through the wall to continue with the
route.*

2. **Bear right at the stone hut, with the drystone wall on your left and
    the woods rising on your right.**

Dolbadarn Castle

3. The path curves around to the right and a building should come into view ahead. Once the building is in sight drop down to the left and follow the fence through the gorse bushes.

4. Go through the kissing gate and follow the grassy path.

☺ On your right now are some ruined buildings. The roofs have collapsed and inside the buildings are overgrown with plants. You can clearly see some of the bricked-up windows and doors.

5. The path curves around to the right and leads you down to a gateway. Go through and bear right along the pavement, passing the hotel.

6. Carefully cross the road and take the turning off to the left, along Victoria Terrace.

Q: You are now passing many houses on your left. One of them has a date on the front. What is the date? It is fairly easy to spot.

A: 1906

7. **Turn right again, signed for the waterfalls. Cross over the river and go under arched railway bridge.**

☺ The bridge you have just walked under carries a railway line which climbs up to the top of Snowdon, the highest mountain in England and Wales. You might be lucky enough to see one of the little steam trains crossing over on its way to the top of the mountain. The trains are a special type that can go uphill. Perhaps you have been to the top on the train. The railway was opened in 1896, over 100 years ago, and it is still very popular today. It takes about an hour to get to the top. It takes a lot longer if you walk, as many people do. You will probably pass many walkers with heavy rucksacks on their way up Snowdon, as one of the popular paths is close by.

8. **Follow the road to the left. Keep left and cross the cattle grid, signed again for the waterfalls.**

9. **Keep left and follow the pathway leading under the viaduct. This will take you all the way to the waterfalls.**

    (*WARNING:* There is a drop down to the water on the left, so keep young children under close control.)

☺ The water is very fast flowing and gushes down from the mountains to join the lake in the valley. The waterfalls are among the most popular in Wales.

10. **From the falls return the same way, under the viaduct, keeping right to the cattle grid, then bearing right onto the lane. Go under the bridge again and bear left along Victoria Terrace. At the end of the road turn left, towards the village centre.**

On the left is the start of the Snowdon Mountain railway, where you can board a train to the summit of Snowdon. Also here there are refreshments and toilets.

Escape route: Cross over the road from the station and follow the road signed for the castle, which will return you to the car park/Starting Point.

11. **Continue past the Snowdon Mountain Railway. Cross over the road and go through the gates and onto the playing fields. Follow the well worn path towards the lake.**

☺ Straight ahead you should be able to see grey stone scars left by quarrying. For many years slate was cut from here, and was carried away by a small railway to the coast.

More information about the Llanberis slate quarries and their history from the Padarn Country Park, which is where this route leads.

12.   **Go through the gate onto the open grassy area. Follow the path as it bears to the right and crosses the small footbridge.**

☺ To the right you should have a good view of the round tower of the castle.

13.   **Follow the path, which starts to bear to the right to a footbridge over the river. Cross over.**

☺ This bridge crosses the river which links the two lakes in the valley: Llyn Padarn to your left, and Llyn Peris to your right. At one time they were both part of the same huge lake, which filled the whole of the valley.

Bear left after the bridge for Padarn Country Park, where you will find toilets, refreshments, museums, lakeside railway and gift shops.

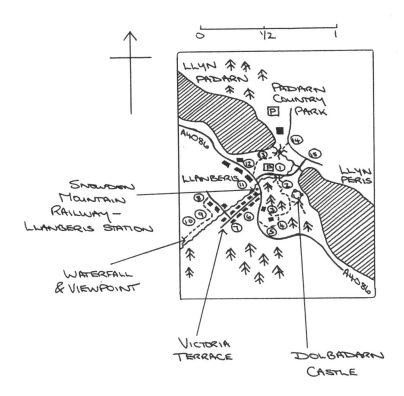

14. **Bear right after the bridge and go through the gateway. Follow the pavement which bears around to the right and crosses the river again.**

☺ On your left is Llyn Peris. In the mountain behind you is a "hydro-electric" power station. "Hydro" means water. Electricity is made by water turning huge "turbines". All this sounds very complicated, but you might find it easier to understand if you visit the Electric Mountain centre, in the village, where you can learn all about the power station.

Electric Mountain can be found in the centre of the village, on the main road, next to the main car park. There are displays and exhibitions, refreshments and toilets, and from here you can book a guided tour into the power station.

15. **Follow the road back to the car park/Starting Point, which is on the right.**

Dolbadarn Castle Checklist

☐ A CASTLE

☐ A SHEEP

☐ A WATERFALL

☐ A BOAT

☐ A TRAIN

☐ SOMEONE WITH A CAMERA

☐ SOMEONE WITH A RUCKSACK

☐ A DOG

☐ A CHURCH TOWER

☐ AN ACORN

☐ A SHOP SELLING POSTCARDS

☐ A WHITE HOUSE

Llanberis: Llyn Padarn

This is quite a long walk, and strenuous in parts on the far side of the lake. A quarter of the route is uphill, a quarter downhill and the rest is completely flat. Starting from the Llanberis side the going is easy and suitable for pushchairs as far as Padarn Country Park. Even less enthusiastic walkers shouldn't have any trouble winding their way up to the Quarry Hospital Café and information centre, after which the going starts to get tougher, so this would be a good point to return the same way to the Starting Point, or spend some time enjoying what the country park has to offer, including the Llanberis Lake Railway. The whole route would take half a day to walk, but it is worth taking longer to enjoy everything that is on offer, including plenty of wildlife and some spectacular views of the area.

Starting Point: The "Village car park" in Llanberis (SH578604) off the A4086, right next to the "Electric Mountain"/information centre. Any of the various car parks in Llanberis would be fine, just head for the lake edge and walk with the water on your left.

By Bus: Services from Caernarfon, Bangor, Betws-Y-Coed and Beddgelert.

Car Parking: Starting Point, or various lay-bys off the main road, or any of several well signed car parks, including at Dolbadarn Castle and at Padarn Country Park.

Distance: 5 miles.

Terrain: On the far side of the lake there are rocky footpaths and quiet lanes. On the Llanberis side the route follows mainly an old railway line and lakeside footpaths, though there are two short stretches along the main road, but there is a wide pavement.

Maps: OS Landranger 115, OS Outdoor Leisure 17.

Public Toilets: At Electric Mountain, Padarn Country Park: near the car park and at the Quarry Hospital.

Refreshments: Electric Mountain, Padarn Country Park, Caffi Padarn on the opposite side.

Q: Look out for a slate plaque at the back of the car park in memory of an American President called Thomas Jefferson. What is the date on the plaque?

A: 3 July 1993

1.   **From the car park cross the bridge over the small stream, go
        through the gate and follow the lakeside path, with the water on
        your left.**

☺   The path leads through an open grassy field where there might be cows
        or sheep. Ahead you should be able to see the round tower of
        Dolbadarn Castle, which is over 800 years old. Further away, some-
        times covered in cloud, is Snowdon, the highest mountain in England
        and Wales.

2.   **Go through/past the stranded kissing gate which currently has no
        fence or wall to accompany it. Continue ahead along the clear
        path.**

☺   In the distance ahead and to the left you should be able to see heaps of
        grey stone, which were once part of the Llanberis slate quarries, which
        closed in 1969. Slate is a hard grey stone which can be used for build-
        ing, and can be split into thin sheets to use for roof tiles. Many of the
        houses in the area are made of local slate. See if you can spot any on
        your walk.

3.   **Cross over the plank bridge and a further small bridge. Continue
        ahead.**

☺   In case you haven't already noticed it, the small hut on your left is made
        of slate.

4.   **Bear left over the concrete and metal footbridge across the river.**

☺   Looking over the bridge you can see the river that connects the two
        lakes in the valley, Llyn Padarn to your left and Llyn Peris to your right.
        The water is very clear, and you should be able to see the slate and
        other stones on the bottom. Can you see any fish?

5.   **Bear left along the pavement.**

Escape route: Bear right and follow the pavement back into the village centre. The car park is on the right after the Electric Mountain Centre.

6.   **Continue along the pavement to Padarn Country Park.**

☺   This is Padarn Country Park, and it is on the site of the old slate quarry.
        From the buildings on your left you might hear the sound of cutting or
        drilling, as it is still used as a slate works. The wall on your left is slate.

Llyn Padarn and Dolbadarn Castle

There are many different types of slate. Notice all the different shades of grey there are in this one wall.

Around the front of this building you will see train sheds, where the small steam trains are kept that run along two miles of trackway along the edge of the lake. This railway line was used for carrying slate, and once ran all the way to the coast.

7.   Cross over the entrance to the car park and follow the railway lines on your right.

The station is on the right for those wishing to take a ride on the steam trains. The toilets are on the left.

8.   Continue ahead at the end of the car park, passing behind the water sports building. Follow the slate trackway leading uphill. Keep ahead, between the low slate walls.

☺   As you get higher there are views across the lake, back towards the castle and the town. Over the rooftops of the houses see if you can spot the church.

At the top of this path there is a grassed area where there are a few

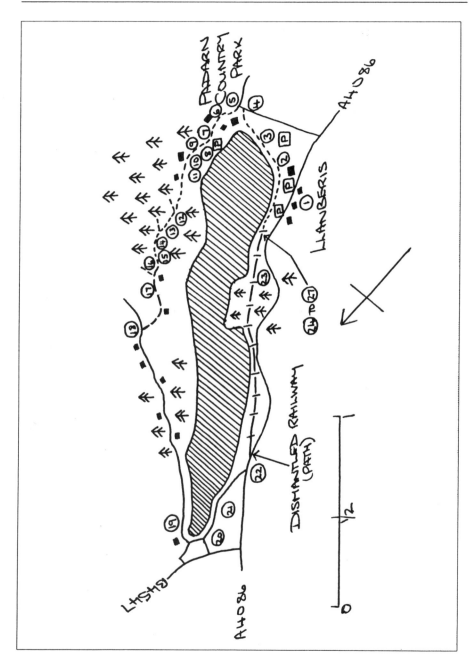

benches where you can sit and rest, or have a picnic. While you are here look for the "Slate Sea" sculpture in the grass. Also, look out for the map of the lake, telling you what all the mountains are called that you can see. See if you can work out which Snowdon is. It is called "Yr Wyddfa" in Welsh, from the Welsh word for grave, because an old legend tells that a giant is buried there.

9. **Follow the path as it leads to the bridge over the railway lines, and follow the steps uphill.**

Q: Look out for a date plaque in the steps. What is the date?

A: 1892

☺ At the top of the steps you will find the Quarry Hospital, which was built to look after the ill and injured amongst the men working at the quarry.

Here there are picnic benches and good views over the lake. Inside the hospital there are displays and exhibits, toilets, refreshments and information.

10. **Facing the Quarry Hospital bear left and follow the path, keeping left towards the woods.**

☺ Just before you come to the woods, you should pass on your right the old "mortuary" which is a place where the dead were laid out. If you dare to look inside, you will see there are two stone slabs for the bodies. A quarry was a very dangerous place to work, and people sometimes got killed in accidents, or died of diseases. The plaque above the door shows the date 1906.

11. **Keep to the left of the mortuary and follow the path leading into the woods.**

Take care now as the path may be rocky and uneven in places. Keep smaller children under close control, as the woods lead quite steeply downhill on the left in some places.

Q: After a short way you will pass an old stone building on your left. If you go inside you will see what looks like a bench with holes cut into it. What do you think this building was?

A: These were the outside toilets for the hospital. Nice.

12. **Avoid the path joining from the right and keep ahead.**

☺ The woods are rising up on the right. The trees at the moment are mainly oaks. On your left, through the trees, you might be able to see the lake, Llyn Padarn, and possibly the tracks of the little steam railway which runs alongside it.

You should soon come to a viewpoint, where you can see over the lake and back over the quarry buildings.

13. **Avoid the path to the right and continue ahead, still uphill, scrambling over stone where necessary. (Beware of the drop to the left.)**

14. **The path starts to descend. Avoid the path to the left, leading downhill. Keep to the main path, which is fairly level at this point.**

☺ You should be able to hear the sound of a waterfall now, which rushes towards the lake, carrying all the water from the hills and mountains.

15. **Go through the kissing gate and bear right along the stream and then cross the stream via the stone slab bridge. Watch your footing.**

☺ Soon a stream should come in sight, which you need to cross over. The path after the stream leads uphill again, I'm afraid. Keep a look out for squirrels and wild rabbits.

16. **Keep ahead, avoiding the path to the right.**

☺ On the right there are old ruined farm buildings. You can see the old doorways and windows. The insides of the buildings are now overgrown with wild plants.

Many of the trees along this part of the path are silver birches. They are easy to spot because they have thin, white trunks. They grow well in rough land like this.

17. **Pass the small car park on the left. Keep straight ahead along the stony trackway. Avoid all footpaths and tracks leading off on either side. Go under the old stone bridge and continue ahead.**

Q: Look out for the cottage on the right. How many chimneys does it have on the main roof?

A: Two.

(On the left you should pass Cwm Derwen, which is a woodland and wildlife centre open to the public. Also here you will find Caffi (café) Padarn, an adventure playground and craft shop.)

18. **The track still leads uphill, but soon becomes a tarmac driveway. At the next bend, if you can spot it, follow the footpath to the left through the undergrowth and up to the lane, bearing left. (If you miss this follow the driveway up to the lane and bear left.) This is a quiet lane, but take care of any possible traffic. The route now follows this lane for 1 mile, so avoid any paths, gates, trackways leading off it.**

☺ That was the last uphill stretch of the walk. From now on it's either down-hill or level. You will be walking along this lane for a mile; here are some things you should pass:

A house on the right with four arched windows.

A post-box in the wall.

An old cottage on the right which has a horseshoe on the door. This is supposed to bring good luck.

Stone walls with ivy growing on them.

Every so often you should get a view of the lake over the treetops on the left.

Q: At the bottom there is a tight bend in the lane, after which you can see the lake is closer. Look ahead to the stone bridge; how many arches has it got?

A: Four.

☺ Look out for the house on the right before the bridge, which has wagon wheels and horse shoes built into the gate.

19. **Keep left and cross over the stone bridge.**

Q: Can you see the round road sign with a coach in the middle? What do you think this means?

A: It means no coaches are allowed down this road.

20. **Keep left after the bridge.**

☺ Look for the sign with a "T" on it. This means the road is a dead end for traffic and doesn't lead anywhere.

21. **Climb the ladder stile and continue along the disused roadway, which passes close to the lake.**

☺ There are good views over the lake from here. Over the water there is a cliff where people often come to rock climb. Perhaps there are some rock climbers there now?

22. **Climb a further ladder stile and continue ahead. At the end of the roadway climb the final ladder stile and bear left, following the pavement. Look out for the gap in the wall on the left and follow the steps leading downhill to a disused railway line. Bear left at the bottom.**

☺ This was once a railway line which ran from Llanberis to Caernarfon. Today it has been made into a path and cycleway, so look out for people on bikes.

Along the path there are many wild plants growing, including ferns, nettles and brambles, and many different trees. Through the trees to the left you should be able to see the lake. See if you can work out where you have walked on the other side of the lake. You might be able to recognise some of the cottages you passed along the lane.

To the right through the trees you should be able to see a pond which was cut off from the main lake where this railway "embankment" was built, which is the raised bank you are walking along. The pond has reeds and lilies growing in it, and is very sheltered because of all the trees around it, so it is very popular with birds and ducks.

23. **Go through the gateway and continue ahead. Opposite the toilet block bear left towards the car park, but then bear immediately right, along a narrow gravel path running parallel with the entrance driveway.**

☺ This path passes through thick bushes, including a bush called "buddleia" which has long clusters of purple flowers. See if you can spot any. The flowers attract butterflies, so it is often called a "butterfly bush". There are many wild rabbits in the area, so keep a look out for a flash of their white tails as they run for cover.

24. **The path opens into a further car park. Follow the white stones. Cross the entrance driveway and again keep with the white stones, back into the trees and bushes.**

☺ Again there are good views of the lake on the left. Can you see any boats on the water?

25. **Join the entrance driveway and keep left, passing Piggery Pottery on your right. Bear left along the pavement of the main road.**

26. **On the left you should come to the first of the Llanberis car parks. At the start of the car park bear left and join the lakeside path.**

☺ This is nearly the end of the walk now. It has been a long walk, but if the weather has been fine you should have seen many interesting and exciting things, including some of the local wildlife.

27. **Keep ahead, passing a playground and picnic area, back to the village car park and Starting Point.**

Llyn Padarn Checklist

☐ A CASTLE

☐ A SEAGULL

☐ A SQUIRREL

☐ AN ACORN

☐ A BOAT

☐ A STONE BRIDGE

☐ A RABBIT

☐ A DUCK

☐ A CHURCH TOWER

☐ A TRAIN

☐ A FIR CONE

☐ A SHEEP

☐ A PLANE

☐ A POSTBOX

Walks around the Mawddach Estuary

The Mawddach Estuary runs, more or less, between Barmouth (Abermaw) and Dolgellau. It is said by many to be the most beautiful part of North Wales.

Barmouth is a functional small town with fine sandy beaches and some seafront amusements and fairground rides. At the harbour there is a ferry across the estuary to Fairbourne, where there is also a good beach and a miniature railway. Also crossing the estuary is a railway/footbridge. There is a small toll charged, but the walk across offers excellent views (see Barmouth to Fairbourne route). Further inland there is a toll road-bridge crossing the afon Mawddach. On the other side is the Mawddach Trail, adapted from a disused railway line, running along the riverside, and the Penmaenpool Nature Centre, housed in an old signal box (see Penmaenpool route). Dolgellau is a neat market town, and well worth a visit. It has a good Tourist Information Centre with free displays and exhibitions.

Looking towards Dolgellau

Mawddach Estuary: Barmouth to Dinas Oleu

A relatively short, but fairly steep walk which offers some good views over the town and further along the beautiful Mawddach Estuary. A good introduction to uphill walking.

Starting Point: The railway station, Barmouth (SH612158). Well signed and right in the middle of the town.

By Rail: Barmouth/Abermaw station, on the Pwllheli to Aberystwyth line.

Car Parking: Various places in the town centre, all well signed.

Distance: Strenuous. Less than a mile, but what this walk lacks for in length it makes up for in height. As the walk is so short there is no Escape Route.

Terrain: Trackways, footpaths and a lot of steps. A great deal of uphill walking.

Maps: OS Landranger 124, OS Outdoor Leisure 18.

Public Toilets: At the station and in the town centre. Well signed.

Refreshments: Various places in the town.

---

1. **From the station head into town, away from the sea. At the main road bear left.**

☺ Look out near the station for the "level crossing", where cars drive across the railway line. When a train is coming the barriers come down to stop the traffic.

You should pass the TIC on your left, which you can pop into for any local information. Towards the end of the road there is a signpost pointing the way to the toilets and various other features and amenities around the town.

☺ You should soon be able to see Saint John's church with its square tower and gold clock, which rises high above the town.

2. **When you see the church on the right, cross the main road and head along the minor road called Saint John's Hill, which bears around to the left below the church.**

☺ Already you are starting to climb up above the rooftops of the lower part of Barmouth, and should soon be able to see the sea in the distance.

Barmouth/Abermaw

There is a lot of climbing in this walk, but the views make it worthwhile. Take your time when walking uphill and make sure you breathe properly, then it won't seem so bad.

3. **Look out for the first turning to the left, which is on the hairpin bend, leading further uphill. Follow this road leading away from the church, and bear right along the signed public footpath, which is narrow and leads uphill. At the top bear right.**

☺ Look out for the water pouring from the mouth of the "mine". A mine is like a cave, except that caves are natural, and mines are man-made, dug out by miners who might be looking for precious metals. There is gold in this part of Wales, though you are unlikely to find any, as it is very rare. The gold for the wedding rings of several members of the Royal Family came from a village near here. Mines can be dangerous, so you should never go inside one. They often have deep holes in the floor, which you might not be able to see in the darkness and might fall into, so stay safe and keep out of mines, no matter how interesting they might look.

You should be able to look down now on the roof of the church. At the

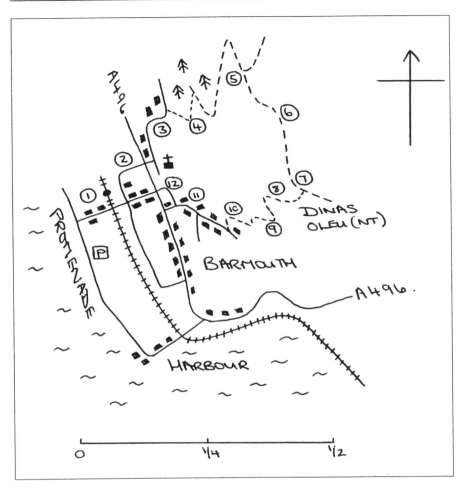

top of the tower there is a "weathervane" in the shape of a cockerel. This shows which way the wind is blowing. Which way is it blowing today?

4. **Go through the metal gate and bear around to the left, following the arrows painted on the rocks.**

☺ There are several bushes growing alongside the path, including gorse, which has sharp thorns and yellow flowers, and also brambles which you probably know quite well, which blackberries come from. The berries start off green and slowly ripen in the sunlight, turning first red, then black.

The path is still climbing, but remember to take your time and enjoy your walk. Look out for another stream coming out of a mine. A mine like this is called a "level", because, quite simply, it is level. A mine that goes straight down into the ground is called a "shaft".

5. **As the stony track bears around to the left keep straight ahead along the clear grassy path which leads more gradually uphill.**

☺ There are good views over the town and out to sea. Look how small the cars and people are now. See if you can spot: a boat out at sea, a bridge over the railway, a red car and someone walking a dog.

6. **Follow the path as it winds around to the left. Go through the open gateway in the drystone wall and continue ahead, then bear to the right along the main pathway which is shored up with stones.**

Q: There are usually many sheep up here. They are quite good climbers and the rocks and steep slopes don't cause them any problems. What do you think sheep mainly eat?

A: That's an easy one. Grass.

7. **Look out for the gate in the wall down on the right. Go through and continue straight ahead, downhill to the seat and shelter.**

☺ This is Dinas Oleu, which was the first piece of land ever given to the National Trust, who came into being originally to protect the shores of Derwent Water, in the Lake District.

Q: It can be quite windy up here, so this bench with the high wall around it makes an ideal place to shelter. What are the two dates carved onto the plaque at the back of the seat?

A: 1895 and 1995. There is a hundred years between these two dates.

☺ The town is still a long way below you. See if you can spot: a railway line, a fairground roundabout, a train, a telephone box and a football pitch.

8. **Pass the shelter on your left and continue downhill, towards the sea, down a couple of steps, then bear right. The path is stepped occasionally.**

☺ Again the church tower should come into view with its clock and its weathervane. Can you tell what the time is by the clock?

9. **The steps wind down quite steeply. Avoid a further set of steps that lead off uphill. Keep heading down at all times.**

☺ Take care going downhill and watch where you put your feet, as it is very easy to slip and fall. If you get bored, you could try counting how many more steps there are to the bottom.

10. **A final set of steps lead you down to a pathway. Bear left, still leading slightly downhill. At the end of the path bear right onto the tarmac lane between the houses. Keep ahead, downhill, avoiding the road off to the left. (The road is quite steep and very narrow. Although there is unlikely to be any traffic, do take care.)**

☺ This is nearly the end of the walk now. Even though it was quite short, you might be tired because of all the climbing, but you don't get such good views without a bit of effort.

11. **Take the right turning just before you reach the main road.**

Q: What is the name of this road?

A: Look for the sign high up on the wall. It is called Water Street.

12. **Follow the road as it bears around to the left and joins the main street. Bear right, and then left, signed for the station.**

Barmouth/Dinas Oleu Checklist

☐ A CHURCH TOWER

☐ A BOAT

☐ SAND DUNES

☐ A BUSH WITH PRICKLES

☐ A WEATHERVANE

☐ A SEAGULL

☐ A TRAIN

☐ A SHEEP

☐ A CAVE OR MINE

☐ A WHITE HOUSE

Mawddach Estuary: Barmouth to Fairbourne

This is a varied and interesting walk and includes an essential trip across the impressive rail and footbridge which spans the mouth of the Mawddach from Barmouth. The walking route isn't actually circular. You can either return the same way, or to round off the trip in style get the train back, which is only two stops and offers a different view of the bridge. Better still, catch the ferry from the Fairbourne side straight back to Barmouth. Do check train and/or ferry times before you begin your walk, so as to avoid disappointment (the ferry operates from Easter to the end of September). The local TIC will be able to sort you out and it's 30 seconds from the Starting Point – head into town from the station and it's on the left. Attractions at Fairbourne include a miniature railway and miles of golden sands, so this walk can make a great day out. The route works equally well in reverse.

Starting Point: Barmouth/Abermaw station (SH612158). Right in the centre of town and well signed.

By Rail: As above. This station is on the Pwllheli to Aberystwyth line.

Car Parking: Massive car parks opposite the sea front. Well signed from the town centre and A496.

Distance: 3½ miles (excluding return trip).

Terrain: This route is completely flat and once out of the town uses footpaths and the seashore.

Maps: OS Landranger 124.

Public Toilets: At the station and at various points in Barmouth. Also at Morfa Mawddach and Fairbourne.

Refreshments: Various places in Barmouth and a few in Fairbourne.

 If you look at the sign at the railway station you will see that this town, like many Welsh holiday places, has two names, an English and a Welsh Name: Barmouth and Abermaw. Notice there is a "level crossing" close to the station, where the road runs across the tracks. When a

The Mawddach estuary and railway/footbridge

train is approaching the barriers come down to stop any cars driving over. If you are lucky you might see them in action.

1. From the station head for the sea front.

There is an amusement arcade and fairground to the right.

2. Bear left along the promenade.

☺ Look to the left and see if you can spot a huge dragon. Can you see it? Above the doors to the Dragon Theatre.

3. As you approach the harbour avoid the right turning along the harbour wall. Continue straight ahead.

☺ There might be boats on your right now, either in water or sand, depending on whether the tide is in or out. Although it might seem strange, the coming and going of the tide is controlled by the moon and the pull it has on the Earth as it circles around us.

4. Pass the café with seats outside and continue along the prom, which curves around to the left.

☺ There are good views from here over the river and out to sea. There is a telescope which will give you a better view of the boats and the opposite side of the river. Telescopes "magnify" things, which makes them appear bigger and nearer.

5.   **Work your way along the harbour, taking care of any ropes or chains that might be stretched across from moored vessels.**

If you haven't already done so, check for times of the ferries at the landing stage.

6.   **Follow the pavement as it passes under the railway bridge. Bear right, following the main road. Cross over when the pavement ends and continue along the other side, passing on your left the unusually named Birmingham Garage.**

7.   **The road now starts to lead out of town. Keep young children under control.**

Q: Look for the triangular sign with a child and a grown-up on it. What do you think it means?

A: Triangular signs are usually warnings for motorists. This one is warning that there might be people, such as yourself, walking on, or trying to cross, the road.

8.   **Carefully cross the road when you see the sign and pathway leading down to the bridge. (There is a toll to cross: 50p for adults, 25p for children) Cross over the bridge.**

☺ Look out for the lifeboat station near the start of the bridge. The boats are launched from underneath where you are standing. They are sent out to rescue people in danger on the sea.

It is quite exciting crossing the bridge which is over half a mile long. You can look over the edge at the water far down below. On your right is the railway line, and a train might slowly pass you on its way across the bridge.

As you get further out there are good views to the left up the river estuary. An "estuary" is the wide part at the end of a river, just before it joins the sea. From here you can see mountains in the distance, and can you see the large house with a tall tower on the roof?

The highest mountain on the other side of the river is called "Cadair Idris". Idris was a giant from a legend, and "cadair" means chair in Welsh, so the mountain is called "Idris's Chair" because it is flat on top and the giant could sit there looking down over the river.

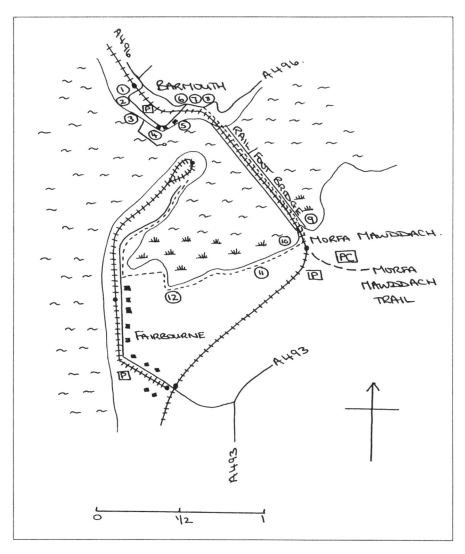

9. **Go through the gate at the end of the bridge and continue ahead along the pathway, still running parallel with the railway.**

☺ On the left is an area of marsh, which might be covered over with water at high tide. As you walk further the land becomes grassier, and there might be sheep grazing.

10. **Keep ahead along the railway and look out for the gate on the right which crosses the railway tracks. Carefully cross over and climb the stile opposite.**

☺ As you probably know, railway lines can be very dangerous, but here the public footpath crosses the tracks. As the sign says, you should "Stop, look and listen" before you cross, to make sure no train is coming. Walk straight across and don't mess about on the railway.

Escape route: Continue up to the platform and catch the train one stop back to Barmouth/Abermaw.

Toilet Emergency? From the platform go through the gate into the car park where you will find a toilet block over on the left, across the Mawddach Trail.

11. **From the stile follow the path, now with the railway on your right. The path then crosses over a stream and bears around to the left. Climb the stile and continue ahead, along the top of the grassy bank, climbing the various stiles ahead.**

☺ On your right you can see over to Barmouth and there are good views of the bridge. There might be a train coming across it. Nearer to there is an area of grassy marsh which is called Morfa Mawddach. "Morfa" is a Welsh word meaning a marsh near the sea. Look out for seagulls and other birds on the marshes.

Q: On the left, because of this high bank you are walking along, the sea is kept off the land, and there are grassy fields where there might be cows or sheep. Do you know what a young cow is called?

A: A calf.

☺ As you walk further, you should be able to see rooftops come into view ahead. This is Fairbourne, which is a little seaside town where there is a miniature railway which you can ride on, and a long, sandy beach to play on.

12. **The path follows the bank for a mile and opens onto a quiet road close to Fairbourne. You now have several options:**

12A. **Bear right along the grass and dunes, following the road and miniature railway line to the ferry terminus, and catch the ferry back to Barmouth.**

12B. **Cross the tracks of the little railway and climb up the steps over the sea wall then bear left for half a mile, enjoy the beach for a** while, then return over the sea wall into Fairbourne, where you will find the station for the little railway and all the usual amenities. Continue along the main street, heading away from the sea, and you will come to the mainline station on the left, where you can catch the train two stops back to Barmouth.

12C. Spend some time on the beach or in Fairbourne, then return the same way along the marshside footpath and across the bridge to Barmouth.

Barmouth and Fairbourne Checklist

- [ ] A BOAT WITH A SAIL
- [ ] A BOAT WITHOUT A SAIL
- [ ] A SEAGULL
- [ ] A FUN FAIR
- [ ] SOMEONE ON A BIKE
- [ ] A WHITE HOUSE
- [ ] SOME SEAWEED
- [ ] A SHEEP
- [ ] A BIG TRAIN
- [ ] A SMALL TRAIN
- [ ] SOME DRIFTWOOD ON THE BEACH
- [ ] A PLANE

Mawddach Estuary: Morfa Mawddach

This walk makes use of an old railway line, now opened as an attractive footpath, called the Mawddach Trail, offering unparalleled views of the Mawddach Estuary. Another bonus is that the walk is almost entirely flat.

Starting Point: Morfa Mawddach Station /car park. (SH142628). Well signed from the A493, a mile north-east of Fairbourne.

By Rail: Morfa Mawddach station, one stop from Barmouth or Fairbourne. Once off the train bear right to the gate into the car park and start from Direction 1.

Car Parking: See Starting Point.

Distance: 2½ miles.

Terrain: The Mawddach Trail is surfaced and flat. The return journey is via footpaths which may be muddy in bad weather. Completely level.

Maps: OS Landranger 124.

Public Toilets: Close to the car park. (Follow Direction 1).

Refreshments: None in the area.

Pushchairs: The Mawddach Trail, being flat, is ideal for pushchairs, but the return route is unsuitable, so after Direction 4 return the same way, or it is possible to continue along the Trail for several miles if you want to extend your walk.

---

1. **From the car park head back towards the entrance and look out for the toilet block over on the left. Here bear right along the flat trackway, which is the Mawddach Trail, passing an information board on your left.**

☺ This was once a railway line, which closed in 1965. Can you work out how long ago that was? Today the tracks have been taken away and the old railway has been made into a popular footpath which runs for nine miles, from Barmouth to Dolgellau. Don't worry, you don't have to walk all that way today. Near here the old line joined the coastal railway, which is still running.

2. **Cross straight over the car park driveway and go through the metal gate opposite, where the Trail continues.**

Morfa Mawddach, coastal marshes

☺ There are trees and blackberry bushes on either side of the path. Many of the trees are silver birch. They are easy to spot because they have slim white "boughs" or "trunks". Some of the trees have ivy on them. Ivy is a climbing plant and can often be found growing up trees, walls or houses. It has tiny suckers so it can stick onto surfaces. Ivy is an evergreen, which means it doesn't lose its leaves in the autumn, like many trees do. Look out in the treetops for birds' nests.

3.   Keep straight ahead along the Trail.

There is a bench and observation point on the right, looking out over the flat fields and marshes.

☺ You should be able to see flat fields on your left, where there will probably be sheep, or perhaps cows. In the distance you can see the countryside which this walk will take you through on the way back.

This part of the railway is raised up on a bank, called an "embankment". This was built because normal trains need to run on level rails. In some places the land is lower, so embankments like this needed to be built. In other places the land is higher, so "cuttings" and tunnels would need to be built.

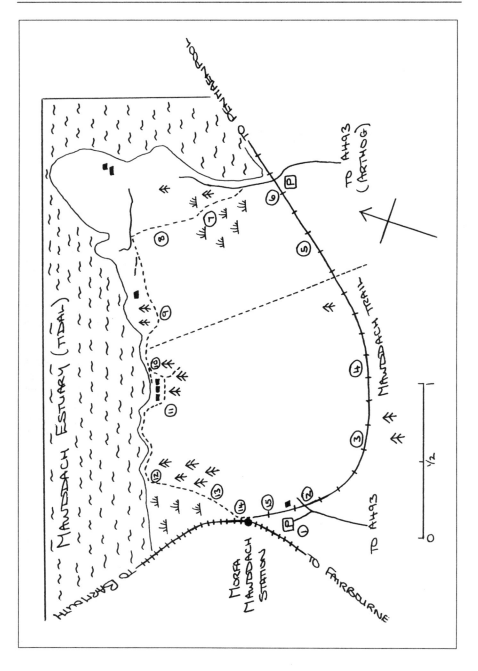

4. **When you come to the gate barring the trackway go through and carry on straight ahead.**

Escape route: This more or less cuts the route in half. Bear left and follow the clear trackway straight ahead across the fields. At the end of the path go through the wooden gate and continue straight ahead to the driveway. Bear left, so the estuary is on your right. Continue from Direction 10.)

☺ To your right you should be able to see the rooftops of a village called Arthog. At one time, a hundred years ago, there were plans to turn Arthog into a seaside village, but it never came about, and today it is a small and fairly quiet place. High up in the hills behind the village are piles of loose slate, which was mined in the area, and at many other places in Wales. For a few years before it closed, slate was carried along this railway.

5. **Pass the small car park on the right and continue ahead, going through the wooden gate barring the trackway. Here bear left along the winding but level, farm driveway.**

6. **Go through the gateway barring the track, signed for a farm. Take the signed footpath off to the left and follow the grassy path between bushes and later trees.**

☺ Look out for bushes along the path which have sharp thorns and yellow flowers. These are called "gorse" and sometimes have a sweet, coconut-like smell. Another type of bush growing nearby, hawthorn, also has thorns. In the winter it has red berries which get eaten by hungry birds and other animals. That doesn't mean the berries are safe for you to eat though. Many wild berries and fruits are poisonous to people, so never eat any.

7. **Although the path winds quite a lot between the trees and bushes it is fairly easy to follow and you shouldn't have any problems. Cross the small metal and concrete footbridge after which the path bears around to the left. There are occasional arrows to point the way.**

☺ There are streams and ditches along the path, some of which might be quite deep, and always remember that water can be dangerous. If you can't already swim you might like to ask about having swimming lessons. Swimming is fun, and could also save your life.

8. **Cross another small footbridge and follow the path straight ahead towards the rocky tree covered mound. Look out for the**

public footpath sign and bear left. (The path at this point is partly covered in concrete strips.) There is another sign and the path becomes grassy. Where the path splits keep to the lower path, signed again as a public footpath.

☺ Over the flat fields on your left you should be able to see Arthog village, with the high hills behind. Keep a look out for wild rabbits, running for cover as you approach.

9.   The path curves around to the right towards fenced woodland. Avoid the path bearing off in front of the woods and continue ahead, passing the woods on your right. The path then bears left and leads you to a metal gateway. Go through the gate, bear right, passing through the wooden gate. Bear left along the driveway, so the estuary is on your right.

☺ This is the afon (River) Mawddach, which joins the sea close by. You should be able to see the wooden bridge crossing the mouth of the river which carries the railway and can also be crossed on foot. The bridge was built in 1876, so it is very old, though it has had a lot of major repair work done on it since then.

There is a little beach here with rocks, sand and seaweed. You might wonder what seaweed is doing in the river, but the sea reaches this far up at high tide. Notice the sign: "Very dangerous currents and channel between high and low tide".

10. When the driveway splits keep left, heading into the woods. (The right turning is private and leads to a strangely isolated row of houses called Mawddach Terrace). Follow the signed footpath to the right, leading behind the houses.

Q: The trees in the woods are "deciduous". Do you know what this means?
A: "Deciduous" trees lose their leaves in the autumn, and new leave grow back again in the spring. Not all trees lose their leaves in the autumn. Those that don't are called "evergreens".

11. The path curves back towards the estuary. Bear left along the clear pathway.

☺ From here you can see the front of the row of houses which look out over the river. They are made of red brick and have lots of chimneys. They are called "Mawddach Terrace" and are named after the river. A terrace is a long row of houses all joined together. Perhaps you live in a house like that.

There is a good view of the railway bridge now. Keep a look out for any trains. Can you see any people walking along the bridge?

12. **The grassy path winds along the estuary and leads you to an area of shale and shingle. Bear around to the left, leaving the river behind.**

☺ During a very high tide parts of the land here may be underwater, so you might find shells on the ground. This is the last part of the walk now.

13. **When you come to the stream straight in front of you bear left, follow the stream to the gate, go through and bear right, so the raised bank is on your right.**

14. **Go through the gate and bear left, which brings you back to the Mawddach Trail again.**
(To return to the station go through the gate on the right, which will lead you directly onto the platform.)

15. **Continue along the trail which will bring you back to the toilets on the left. Bear right for the car park/starting point.**

Morfa Mawddach Checklist

☐ A SEAGULL

☐ A SHEEP

☐ A BRIDGE

☐ SOMEONE ON A MOUNTAIN BIKE

☐ A BOAT

☐ A TRAIN

☐ A WHITE HOUSE

☐ A STONE HOUSE

☐ A METAL GATE

☐ A WOODEN GATE

☐ A YELLOW FLOWER

☐ A WHITE FLOWER

Mawddach Estuary: Penmaenpool

Another walk making use of part of the old railway now known as the
Mawddach Trail, running along the estuary. The return section of the
walk is via footpaths through wild and lonely uplands in the shadow of
the mighty Cadair Idris. At Penmaenpool itself is a nature reserve with
views across the estuary marshes and an observation hide in an old
signal box. A varied and interesting walk.

Starting Point: The car park at Penmaenpool (SH695185), off the A493 signed
for the Abermaw/Barmouth Toll and Nature Centre.

By Bus: Bus services along the A493 between Fairbourne and Dolgellau.

Car Parking: At the Starting Point.

Distance: Moderate/Strenuous. 6 miles, with no Escape Route.

Terrain: Flat trackways on the outward journey, with fairly long ascent on the return journey.

Maps: OS Landranger 124, OS Outdoor Leisure 18

Public Toilets: In the car park, including disabled.

Refreshments: George III pub, with seats outside overlooking the river, close to
the Starting Point.

Pushchairs: The first half of the walk along the Mawddach trail is ideal for
pushchairs, though the return section is unsuitable, so return the same way any
time before Direction 5, or to extend your walk, continue ahead along the Trail.

1. **Head through the car park so the river is on the right. (Here you
    will find toilets and a picnic area. The Nature Centre is open at
    weekends from Easter to May, and daily from June to Septem-
    ber.)**

Q: These marshes along the edges of the river attract a lot of wildlife,
    including herons. What is a heron?

A: A large bird with long legs, which can often be seen standing in shallow
    water. If you look carefully, you might be able to see one.

2. **Carefully cross the driveway to the toll bridge and continue along
    the riverside. (This driveway is used for access only, but be
    aware of any traffic.)**

Looking down on Penmaenpool, the river and toll bridge

☺ This wooden bridge crosses the afon (River) Mawddach. It is a "toll bridge", which means you have to pay to go across. Perhaps there are cars driving across it now? A bit further along you should pass a railway signal by the side of the driveway. This may seem a bit out of place, but this was once an old railway line which was closed in 1965. The bird-hide near the car park was once a signal box and to the left you should be able to see the old railway sign for Penmaenpool station.

Q: What is the name of the white pub?

A: George III, after one of the Kings of England.

(There is outdoor seating at the pub, and good views across the river.)

3. The tarmac drive becomes a stony trackway. Continue ahead, along the Mawddach Trail, avoiding the stile leading off to the right.

Q: You should pass a gushing stream heading down into the river, and soon after you will pass two houses on your left. What is the name of the white one?

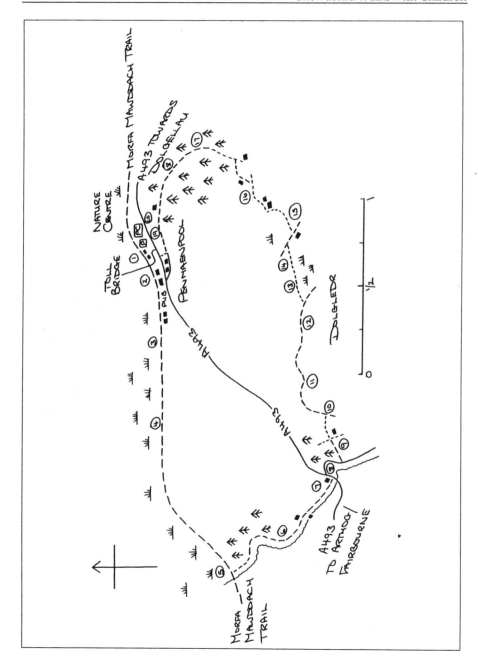

A: Victoria Villa. There is a sign near the front door. A "villa" is a type of house.

4.   Go through the metal gate barring the trackway and continue ahead. Avoid all gates and stick to the Trail for almost a mile and a half.

☺ Notice there are high banks on either side, which are covered in trees and bushes. This is called a "cutting" because a pathway had to be cut through here for the tracks of the old railway.

The cutting soon ends and there are views over the river estuary. The path is now raised up on a bank. This is called an "embankment", and it was built to keep the rails level. A lot of the land around you is marshy and water-logged, though there may still be sheep or cows in the fields.

There are occasional picnic tables along the side of the Trail.

☺ This part of the river is the "estuary", which is the last part before the river joins the sea. Estuaries are usually wide, and tidal, which means the sea comes up them at high tide. In fact, the sea can reach across the marshes to this embankment. If you look at the fence at the bottom of the bank there might be seaweed caught on the wire. There is usually a line of reeds and driftwood which shows how high the tide reaches but don't worry, there isn't much chance of it reaching the pathway.

There should soon be good views to the end of the estuary, where a railway bridge crosses the river. Can you see it? A lot of the hills surrounding the river are covered with trees and are very attractive. Look for the village on the other side of the river, with the houses rising into the trees. This is Bontddu, where the gold for several of the Royal Family's wedding rings has come from. Sometimes gold can be washed down from the mountains and found in and around the river, so keep your eyes open, you never know! In between looking for gold see if you can spot any seagulls or other birds on the marshes.

Soon the old railway crosses a bridge over the clear water of the Afon (River) Gwynant. Can you see any fish in the water?

5.   Bear left down the track BEFORE the bridge and follow the trackway leading upstream, so the river is on your right.

(PUSHCHAIRS and anyone who's getting weary: return the same way along the Mawddach Trail to the Starting Point.)

☺ The path is now passing through the ground of an outdoor pursuits centre, where people learn how to rock climb and canoe. There are often groups canoeing on the river. They will probably have colourful water-proof clothing on and safety helmets.

6.   **Follow the track along the river and when it bears to the right go through the metal gate, signed with arrows. Keep with the river at all times. Follow the track and go through a further gateway and bear right along the farm driveway, still with the river. (Beware now of farm vehicles.)**

☺ In the spring there are daffodils growing along the edge of the river. Look out also for a tall tree on your right, called a redwood, which has a very wide trunk. In America some of these trees have grown so big that holes have been cut in them for cars to drive through. Fortunately, this tree hasn't been damaged in such a way.

Soon a stone arched bridge should come into view ahead, which carries a road over the river.

7.   **At the end of the driveway, taking great care, bear left onto the road. Cross over when safe and bear right, uphill, signed for a Youth Hostel.**

8.   **The lane curves uphill steadily. Pass the "Give Way" sign and about 12 yards after it bear left, uphill towards the metal gate. Don't go through the gate, but bear left, steeply uphill and climb the stile over the fence in front of you. You should now be on a footpath between a wall on the right and fenced woodland on the left. Keep with the wall and don't stray into the woods.**

Q: There are many "conifers" in the woods on your left. Do you know what a conifer is?

A: It is a tree which has its seeds in cones, and has dark needles instead of flat leaves. Can you tell which trees are conifers and which are not? Also, look on the ground for any cones and see how many different types you can find.

9.   **Keep ahead to the top where there is a crossroads of footpaths. Continue straight ahead, crossing the ladder stile. Again keep straight ahead, still with a wall on your right, passing various farm buildings.**

☺ In the summer these hills are covered with bracken, which is a type of fern. In the autumn it turns a yellow or brown colour and dries up but new green shoot will sprout from the ground in the spring. Look out for net-tles also along this part of the path, which, of course, can sting you.

10. **Bear left along the stony farm trackway and follow this as it winds its way uphill through several gateways. Keep with the main trackway at all times.**

☺ There are usually many sheep around here. In the summer they might be hiding amongst the bracken. They eat grass mainly, so there is plenty of food here for them.

Look out for two bushes with prickles. Gorse is very dark and has yellow flowers for most of the year. Hawthorn has pink or white blossom in spring and red berries in the winter. Both these bushes can survive well in cold windy places like this and they make good places for wild animals, like rabbits, to shelter.

As the path climbs higher you should be able to see loose stone at the tops of the hills and looking back there are views over the forest treetops across the river towards Barmouth.

11. **Go over the ladder stile next to the gate and continue with the trackway. There is now a drystone wall on the left.**

☺ A small stream passes under the trackway, carrying water from the hills down to the river below. All rivers lead to the sea. This one, the Mawddach, joins the sea near Barmouth.

Apart from there being gold in these hills, there is also "quartz" which is a nice looking but fairly common white stone. If you look amongst the stones on the trackway you should be able to see several pieces of it. Gold, like many metals, is found in the ground and is dug out of 'mines'. If you look up to the right, amongst all the loose stones, you should see the entrances to two small mines. Mines and caves can be very dangerous, so never go inside them.

Still the track is climbing, but not very steeply now. As you get higher still you should be able to look back and see the long railway bridge crossing the mouth of the river. Perhaps you have been across it on a train or on foot. You might also be able to see cars on the road on the other side of the river. They are so far away they look very small, and you cannot hear the noise of their engines.

The higher you get, the colder and windier it gets. Imagine what it would be like at night, or in the very coldest part of winter. You might be pleased to hear that this is the highest part of the walk now, and it is downhill nearly all the way back.

12. **When the path levels out and there is a drystone wall on your immediate left look out for the stile. Cross over and continue along the well-worn grassy path, leading downhill.**

☺ Take care not to stray from the path, as there is an area of swamp to your right, and if you step in it the water would probably come over the top of your boots, even if you're wearing wellies. The tall grass growing in the marsh is a type of grassy reed, and it grows in very wet places, so it is a good way of telling if a place is going to be water-logged.

As the path leads further downhill you should be able to see rooftops in the distance straight ahead. This is the town of Dolgellau.

13. Avoid the narrow metal gate with the stile next to the stream. Continue past there, straight ahead, and you will come to a long metal gate and a ladder stile over a drystone wall. Climb over and continue ahead downhill with the wall on your right.

☺ You should be able to see the river straight ahead, and in the distance are very high mountains, which might have snow on them, even in fine weather.

14. At the end of the field go through the open gateway in the crumbling wall and follow the trackway to the right, crossing the stream via the small plank bridge. Go through the gate or over the ladder stile and continue along the gravel trackway.

☺ There is a small pond below on the left, then farm buildings come into view. In winter there will probably be smoke coming from the chimneys of the farmhouse.

15. Just before the old barn bear left, downhill towards the farm buildings. Go through the gateway at the back of the farm and follow the trackway leading towards the farmhouse, but bear left before it, going through another gateway and follow the rough trackway.

☺ While walking through this farming land, see if you can spot a farmer in his tractor. Tractors are very powerful and can be used for pulling heavy farm machinery. Because they have such big wheels they can also go up steep hills and through mud which there is plenty of around here after rain.

16. Keep with this trackway, which begins to wind downhill, passing another old stone barn on your left, and leads you down to a gateway. Go through and keep with the trackway, still leading downhill, into the forest.

☺ You are now walking through a forest. The trees are mainly conifers, so look out again for fir cones on the ground. In some areas the trees may have been cut down for their wood. In other parts of the forest new trees will have been planted. Conifers grow quite quickly, and their tall, straight trunks are ideal for cutting into wooden planks, which can be used for building, making furniture and even paper. How many things can you think of in your house which are made of wood?

17. Avoid the track to the right before the pond. Continue ahead.

☺ At the pond there are reeds and other water-loving plants growing around the edges. You might see ducks or frogs, or even a water-vole, which is a small mouse-like creature. Several streams bring water down from the high hills and mountains and empty into the pond. Another stream leaves the pond and flows close to the trackway. This takes the water down to the river. You crossed over this stream near the George III hotel at the start of the walk. Can you remember?

Q: The old stone wall to the right of the path is covered with plants, including moss, ivy, brambles and ferns. Which of these plants has prickles?

A: Brambles have prickles.

☺ As the path gets lower you should be able to see rooftops between the trees to the right.

18. Avoid the metal gateways to the right and continue ahead. Join the driveway, bearing left. Take care of any approaching vehicles now.

☺ There are views to the right through the tall trees to the river and the marshes. Also you should be able to see the toll bridge and then the car park, where the walk started, so now you know the walk is almost over.

19. Look out for the small metal gate in the wall on the right, signed as a public path. Follow the clear pathway downhill through the undergrowth.

20. Bear right along the road. (It is safest to cross as soon as possible, passing the back of the George III, after which the pavement begins.) Bear left and follow the road back down to the car park.

Penmaenpool Checklist

- [ ] A HERON
- [ ] A RAILWAY SIGNAL
- [ ] A BRIDGE
- [ ] A SEAGULL
- [ ] A MOUNTAIN TOP COVERED IN SNOW
- [ ] A COW
- [ ] A BOAT
- [ ] A HORSE
- [ ] A FIRCONE
- [ ] A SHEEP
- [ ] A TRACTOR
- [ ] A DUCK
- [ ] A WHITE STONE
- [ ] A DAFFODIL (IN SPRING)

50 Questions & Answers for Boring Journeys

Some are as easy as falling off a Welsh log. Some are harder. Many of the answers can be found within the pages of this book.

Wales
1. What is the highest mountain in Wales?
2. Which white and green vegetable is the emblem of Wales, and can be found on a pound coin?
3. Which mythical animal can be found on the Welsh flag?
4. Which of the Queen's sons is known as the Prince of Wales?
5. What is the name of the dog who was supposed to be buried at Beddgelert?
6. Which grey stone (often used for roofing) is quarried in many places in Wales?
7. Which Welsh seaside town would you go to visit "the Littlest House"?
8. The name of which Welsh village means "the church in the woods?"
9. Which one of these ISN'T a Welsh town? Caernarfon, Chester, Porthmadog.
10. Which of these IS a Welsh island? The Isle of Man, the Isle of Wight, Anglesey.

True or False?
11. There are castles at Conwy, Caernarfon and Harlech.
12. There is a song called "Men of Harlech".
13. You can drive through a tunnel under the river at Conwy.
14. The Mawddach, the Conwy and the Artro are all the names of Welsh rivers.
15. "Bara brith" is a special type of Welsh mountain sheep.
16. There is a railway along the edge of the lake at Bala.
17. There is a power station inside a mountain at Llanberis.
18. Blaenau Ffestiniog is famous for its pottery.
19. You can go skiing in Snowdonia.
20. Snowdon is famous for being the birthplace of King Arthur.

Welsh words
What do these words mean?
21. Aber
22. Castell
23. Araf
24. Newydd
25. Pont

Nature
26. Which birds are known for stealing shiny objects?
27. From which tree do conkers come from?
28. What is a Red Admiral?
29. What is a baby duck called?
30. Some birds "migrate" in winter. What does this mean?
31. What is a "deciduous" tree?
32. What is a "conifer"?
33. How many "toes" does a cow have?
34. Some animals, like hedgehogs, "hibernate" in the winter. What does that mean?
35. Which small bird is famous for its red chest?

General Knowledge
36. Can you name the four points of the compass?
37. Which way does the needle on a compass always point?
38. Who lives at 10 Downing Street?
39. Which children's programme has got a colour and a boy's name in the title?
40. Do you know what glass is made from? (There is a lot of it near the sea).
41. What colour do you get by mixing yellow and blue paint?
42. In Britain, do cars drive on the right or the left of the road?
43. What type of book has the meaning of words in it?
44. In which country do the men traditionally wear kilts?
45. How many sides are there to a rectangle?
46. What is the name of the Queen's only daughter?
47. Do you know what the capital of France is?
48. How many pennies are there in a pound?
49. What language do they speak in America?
50. How many sides does a fifty pence have?

Answers

Wales

1. Snowdon
2. The leek
3. A red dragon
4. Prince Charles
5. Gelert
6. Slate
7. Conwy
8. Betws-y-Coed
9. Chester is in England
10. Anglesey

True or False

11. True
12. True
13. True
14. True
15. False. It is a type of fruity loaf
16. True
17. True
18. False. It is famous for its slate and slate caverns
19. True. There is a dry ski slope near Capel Curig
20. False

Welsh Words

21. River mouth
22. Castle
23. Slow
24. New
25. Bridge

Nature

26. A magpie
27. Horse chestnut
28. A butterfly
29. A duckling
30. They fly south to warmer countries
31. It loses its leaves in winter
32. It has cones which carry its seeds and they also have needles instead of flat leaves.
33. Two, or rather each hoof is split in two.
34. They go to sleep until the spring.
35. A robin, or robin red breast.

General Knowledge
36. North, south, east and west
37. North
38. The Prime Minister
39. Blue Peter
40. Sand
41. Green
42. Left
43. A dictionary
44. Scotland
45. Four
46. Princess Anne
47. Paris
48. One hundred
49. English
50. Seven

Games for long journeys

1. If you are in a car, you will pass may road signs. Oh, the fun that can be had guessing what each sign means. (Useful for adult drivers as well!) Might also come in handy later in life.

2. Think of a subject, e.g.: animals, birds, trees and each child or member of the party has to say a type of animal. After a few rounds it will get more difficult. If you can't answer you are out. The winner, obviously, is the one remaining at the end.

3. I-Spy, an old favourite and a cure for insomnia.

4. Guess Who? Think of a famous person, cartoon character etc and the children have to guess who is it by asking questions, such as: are you a woman? Are you on television? Give them the odd clue occasionally to help them along.

5. Counting things. On a car journey, the most obvious subject would be cars. Each person picks a different coloured car, the winner is the one who has pointed out the most at the end of the journey.